CW01083784

ESSENTIAL QUESTIONS TO ASK WHEN BUYING A PROPERTY IN SPAIN

Tom Provan

ESSENTIAL QUESTIONS TO ASK WHEN BUYING A PROPERTY IN SPAIN

Tom Provan

summersdale

ESSENTIAL QUESTIONS TO ASK WHEN BUYING A PROPERTY
IN SPAIN

Copyright © Tom Provan, 2008

All rights reserved.

No part of this book may be reproduced by any means, nor transmitted, nor translated into a machine language, without the written permission of the publishers.

The right of Tom Provan to be identified as the author of this work has been asserted in accordance with sections 77 and 78 of the Copyright, Designs and Patents Act 1988.

Condition of Sale
This book is sold subject to the condition that it shall not, by way of trade or otherwise, be lent, re-sold, hired out or otherwise circulated in any form of binding or cover other than that in which it is published and without a similar condition including this condition being imposed on the subsequent publisher.

Summersdale Publishers Ltd
46 West Street
Chichester
West Sussex
PO19 1RP
UK

www.summersdale.com

Printed and bound in Great Britain

ISBN: 978-1-84024-640-7

Acknowledgements

I would like to acknowledge the help and support I have received from my many friends in Spain who have always been there during the research and writing of this book and helped me fill the gaps in my knowledge. In particular, I would like to thank Mercedes Enriques de Salamanca who has always been a wonderful source of Spanish knowledge and Lynda Proud who is the friendly estate agent mentioned several times in the book. Without her our life in Spain, especially in the early days, could have been far more difficult.

I would also like to thank Jennifer Barclay of Summersdale for giving me the opportunity to write this book and to the editors, designers and printers who have transformed my words into a finished publication.

Many books have been written about relocating to Spain. Many are excellent, although some could have benefited from more thorough research. I have tried to ensure that all the information in the following pages has been thoroughly checked for accuracy. To that end, I have used a variety of resources, including many other publications and websites and I would like to extend my thanks to them and those who prepared the information.

Finally, I would like to acknowledge the support of my partner without whose encouragement this book might never have been finished.

Contents

Introduction

During the last eight years, my partner and I have bought and sold two properties in Spain. We have viewed many more and made offers on several others. We have helped and advised many friends who wanted to buy a holiday home or a permanent residence in Spain. With the benefit of hindsight there are decisions which we might not have made and different paths which we might have followed. I hope that this book will help you to make the right decisions and avoid the mistakes of those who have come before you, whether you're looking for a good investment, a home from home or a brand new life in the sun.

Our first Spanish property purchase came about when we had reached the stage in life which faces many people nowadays - early retirement. Our employers had made us offers we could not refuse and we were getting too old to start another career. In addition, we realised there was considerable equity in our home in the UK in which we had lived for many years. However, this property was in south-west London and had high overheads if we counted the cost of the tail-end of a mortgage, council tax and utility bills plus the high cost of living on the outskirts of London.

When we did the simple arithmetic we realised that we could sell our UK property and enjoy the proceeds of our hard work thanks to the increased value of our UK property. We could move to somewhere less expensive in the UK or we could move abroad. Spain appeared to be the logical choice for people in our situation.

We had always enjoyed holidays in Spain, especially as the climate, particularly in the south-east and south-west, close to the sea, is considerably better than in the UK. In fact, the World Health Organisation (WHO) regards the Costa Blanca and the Costa del Sol as two of the healthiest environments in the world in terms of air quality. We already knew many people who lived either permanently or semi-permanently in the south-west of the country, along the Costa del Sol, so the decision was made. Spain it would be!

One thing which I pride myself on is that I never make decisions without a great deal of investigation beforehand. I have a very enquiring mind and continue to follow up all my decisions even after they have been made. Although I already had friends who lived in Spain, I did not take their encouragement at face value. I double-checked any statement they made and armed myself with reference books which would help, as well as checking things out on the Internet.

Thanks to this wonder of modern technology, I accessed many websites and was able to investigate many different areas, not just those in which we had friends. I also checked out many of the estate agents in southern Spain who advertise on the Internet and in mid-2000, we set off on our first trip to actually view property. It was an exciting visit and at that time property in Spain still appeared to be ridiculously cheap compared to prices in south-west London. Prices have risen considerably since then.

During that first trip we actually made an offer on a new build apartment, despite the fact that we had actually wanted an older property. On this occasion, I allowed my heart to rule my head. I did not listen to friends who already lived in Spain, or to my own advice which I would now give to everyone – always rent first. We returned to the UK to tell all our friends that we had found perfection. Thanks to a persuasive estate agent we were able to pay the initial deposit using a UK credit card in order to secure this 'dream' property.

Only later did we find out that we had actually made a terrible mistake and we had to pull out. We only discovered this because we asked the right questions and had a very good independent Spanish lawyer. He worked his way through the legal documents and advised us against the purchase. He actually managed to get our deposit back, minus his fees of course, and had we not used his services, we might have made a terrible mistake.

This first apartment was, or appeared to be, wonderful at the time. It was in the first phase of a new development with spectacular views over the Mediterranean and, at the time, nothing obstructed those views. Several years later it is hidden by new developments, and the views have disappeared. The entire area looks like one of the new towns built in Britain during the 1960s and 1970s.

We then found an alternative property in an established urbanisation through a very good local estate agent, who has subsequently become a good friend, and we made an offer.

This offer went through and we bought a resale apartment in an established urbanisation on bridging finance from our bank in the UK for £65,000. This was our first Spanish property and would be our stepping stone to our present home in Spain.

We used this property for several holidays which were also combined with other inspection trips to find our second property. We finally moved in to this property after we had sold our house in the UK.

After an exhaustive search we found a second property in Spain so that the first could be used as a letting investment, which initially was very successful. We looked at many types of property; small villas, village houses, country houses, *fincas* (farmhouses), and apartments. Believe it or not, we ended up buying a second, larger apartment in an urbanisation just down the road from our first property. This was convenient because it meant that we could easily manage the rentals.

By the end of 2001 we were resident in Spain with no property in the UK. We also had potential rental income from the first property which would hopefully augment our income from pensions and investments in the UK.

Based on my experiences and my continued interest in property in Spain, the following pages will, I hope, provide you with a wide range of important information to help you make the right decisions and encourage you to carry out your own investigations. I have included many different sources of information to help you, whether you choose to use the Internet or ask those who have already bought property or seek advice from the appropriate professionals.

You would never buy a property in the UK without doing your homework, but unfortunately many people have been seduced into buying a Spanish property almost in the same way that they buy a souvenir of their holiday. This was particularly true when properties were much cheaper. There was a time when a Spanish property could have been purchased using a relatively small bank loan rather than a mortgage. Many of these buyers have had no problems, but there are some who have had real problems because they did not do the same kind of homework they would do at home.

There are many questions which you must ask. Some are questions you must ask yourself, others are questions for estate agents, lawyers and the authorities in Spain. If you make the decision to buy property in Spain you will be buying in a foreign country, even though it is a part of the European Union (EU). There are different procedures which need to be followed and different laws which need to be taken into account.

There may be points in the book where you might think I am being unduly negative. This certainly isn't my intention; I simply hope to make you think so that you can avoid some of the problems which have faced others in the past because they have not asked the right questions. You can learn from their experiences and transform your buying experience into something really positive which will be successful for you in the long term.

I have tried to organise this book chronologically, taking you through the various stages of the property buying process. There are many other books on the market which will provide you with further information and are worth investing in. The small expense of providing yourself with the right information is worthwhile if you're planning such a major investment as buying a property in Spain. There are also plenty of excellent websites which will give you access to a wealth of information in the comfort of your own home – just perform an Internet search on living in Spain.

I have provided a glossary of words and terms which you might encounter in your various investigations together with a description and translation of the words and terms found on the *escritura* (Spanish title deeds) which you will come across when buying property.

At the end of each chapter there is a summary of the questions which you should ask yourself or the professionals who are working for you.

If you do your research thoroughly and ask the right questions, the experience of buying a property in Spain will be positive and your future life could be wonderful. If you rush into decisions without asking these essential questions at all or do not have the right people to advise you, you could make some expensive mistakes. It's not worth losing out financially and ruining the opportunity that you have because you were ill-informed and unprepared. Spain has so much to offer either as a holiday destination or as a new home, so why not make the most of it?

Chapter 1
Why do I want to buy a property in Spain?

Today there are several million British citizens who have chosen to relocate from the UK and many more are considering a similar move.

Recent figures in a BBC survey suggest that almost 10 per cent of British citizens now live permanently outside the UK and Spain is the second most popular destination after Australia. If you want to check these figures for yourself and you have access to the Internet, simply go to www.bbc.co.uk/news and in the search box type in 'emigration figures'. Other surveys suggest that there are several million more UK inhabitants who are considering a move abroad. Is modern Britain such a terrible place to live and are the British so easily swayed by the power of the media and its portrayal of a new and better life in the sun?

The first stop for many people is a Spanish property exhibition. This can be a very valuable way to learn about various regions with property for sale, but remember, these exhibitions are heavily supported by developers, all of whom, naturally, have a strong vested interest in selling their new properties, not just in Spain but increasingly in Eastern Europe. Their sales techniques can be very persuasive and they have the right contacts to help you raise the necessary finance. The trick is not to be seduced by TV shows and property exhibitions. The life of an expat is not always the bed of roses that many relocation programmes would have you believe. Although some people do find their 'dream' home at what appears to be a bargain price, you must personally investigate each area and you certainly should not sign anything or pay any deposit on a property without seeing it first.

More recently, a new type of relocation TV programme has appeared which actually helps people return to Britain. Yet if you carefully consider all the options available and address the questions raised in this book you're unlikely to have any regrets and won't want to return.

 ## 'Why Spain?'

Why not Spain? The country is wonderful and full of history. The climate is far better than in the UK although the centre can be very cold in winter. Madrid is the highest capital city in Europe, and the north-west of the country can be very wet at any time of the year because its climate is influenced by the Atlantic. On the Costas, there are on average over 300 days of sunshine a year but many of the remaining days can be very wet, the temperatures though are normally much higher than in the UK.

The country is far larger than Britain with a smaller population of just over 40 million, so there are vast areas which are under-populated – although you might not realise this if you have never visited inland Spain. Politically, the country is a democratic monarchy with a federal system of government. It's divided into 17 self-governing regions, known as autonomous communities, which are basically free to make their own laws although Madrid acts for everything which represents Spain in the outside world. Spain is now a modern western European democracy, in which the various laws defined by the EU make it a safe place to invest your hard earned cash in property.

The coastal areas can often appear to be almost over-populated, particularly in the summer months when these areas are buzzing. However, if you long for peace and quiet then inland Spain is probably one of the most interesting areas of Europe – and it's still within easy reach of the UK.

Almost 77 per cent of Spain's population lives on the coast, in Madrid or in other urban areas. So if you drive north on the coastal motorway from the Costa del Sol to Perpignan in France, Spain appears to be a very busy country. More than 80 per cent of the land mass of the country is inland, yet only 23 per cent of the population live in this vast area. With the exception of the area around Madrid, you can drive for miles on inland Spanish motorways and see virtually no cars.

Most expats are attracted to coastal areas such as the Costa Brava, Costa Dorada, Costa Blanca, and the Costa del Sol. Very few new foreign residents move to inland Spain, what some call the real Spain, where life really does progress at a much slower pace.

Spain's National Institute for Statistics (INE) published figures in 2003 (latest available figures) which stated that there were just under 2.7 million (legal) foreigners living in Spain. Of these almost 88 per cent live on the coast, in the Madrid region or on the Balearic and Canary Islands. There is probably the same number of immigrants living on the Costas without official registration. Many of our friends aren't registered with the Spanish authorities. There is further information available in English on the INE website, www.ine.es (although the site is not easy to navigate), or on www.euroresidentes.com.

For many, coastal Spain has always been and will continue to be an absolute paradise. There are very few countries where it's possible to move to a wonderful new home and be able to get away with learning little, if any, of the language. It's true that in the coastal areas virtually all the restaurants have English-speaking staff – and the Spanish staff want to speak English because it is good for the tourist industry. Menus are usually printed in Spanish, English, German and French. When you need a tradesman you will be able to find a British expat who already lives there plying his trade, although you should make sure he is legal. The staff in the bank speak English, and you will be able to find an English-speaking doctor, lawyer, financial adviser, architect, or any other professional you might need. I know people in coastal Spain who have lived there for almost twenty years and still can't count beyond three in Spanish because they don't need to. However, bear in mind that not learning any Spanish will limit your experiences in Spain and may cause you problems if you can't communicate in an emergency. I have covered this in more detail later in the chapter.

Of all legal (registered) immigrants, only 50,000 live in Spain's rural areas (official figures covering all nationalities). So if you decide that you really want to live in rural Spain – more than 100 kilometres from the coast – the chances of having a neighbour from your country of origin are very remote indeed. If you're one of the few people who decide that a new life in the Spanish countryside is for you, then an ability to speak or understand Spanish will be much more important, and in some cases absolutely vital. In the north-east of Spain (the region of Catalonia), it's a good idea to at least have a working knowledge of Catalan, the region's official language. 16 per cent of the population speak Catalan as a first language, forms and official paperwork may only be available in Catalan and the language is taught as a first language in local schools. In addition, you should also be fairly fluent in Castilian Spanish.

Our first Spanish home was close to a beautiful *pueblo blanco* (white village), Casares. Its population is around 90 per cent Spanish, an ability to speak the language there is important, whereas another stunning *pueblo blanco*, Gaucín, is already almost 50 per cent colonised by the Brits and therefore English is widely spoken. Further along the coast there is a joke about another similar town, Mijas, where it is often said that the only people who speak Spanish are the cleaners and the gardeners.

So if you are from the UK and you want to relocate to a country where the climate is better than the UK, and property is still relatively cheap (as long as you stay away from the property hotspots), the cost of living is still reasonable but you might be worried about learning a new language, then coastal Spain is absolutely ideal.

If you want to really experience a new environment, are prepared to learn the language and integrate into a Spanish community, then inland Spain may be for you. Property prices inland remain competitive, and the cost of living is very low with many people growing their own food or buying at local markets. You can still live the simple country life and live in an economically prosperous, developed EU country.

'How has the Spanish property market developed in recent years?'

The market has been through some ups and downs since the severe slump of the early 1990s. It recovered in the mid-1990s and the market was very buoyant in the coastal regions of Spain until about 2003. In fact, Spanish property prices increased more rapidly than in virtually any other EU country. Country property in remote rural areas did not increase quite so dramatically.

Much interest was shown in rural property following the publication of *Driving over Lemons,* which described a lyrical return to nature in a small Spanish *finca* in the Alpujarras, a mountainous inland area south of Granada. Often the local population resent books of this type because they usually push up local property prices and put them out of reach of the locals.

During the last 10–15 years an amazing number of new properties have been built on the Spanish Costas. This is particularly true in Andalusia and in Valencia, where Torrevieja is often referred to as the largest building site in Europe. It has also led to new developments in Murcia and on the Costa de la Luz in western Andalusia.

Many sales have been funded by the overall buoyancy of European property markets. In northern Europe, homeowners found that they could re-mortgage their homes to release equity and buy a holiday property in Spain. Alternatively, if they sold up totally in their home country they could afford to buy a wonderful Spanish home and start a new life in the sun on the proceeds. Sales have also been encouraged by the relatively low rates of interest on mortgages in the Eurozone.

Many observers thought this could not last indefinitely and even when we first bought property in 2001, we were warned that the bubble was about to burst. Some agents actually recommended that we wait a year before buying because prices were about to drop. It did not happen so I am pleased that we bought when we did. Our first property appreciated by more than 60 per cent in two years, partly helped by the fact that the prices of new property were being driven up by the developers.

Then around 2004 the market did start to slow up. When we sold our second property the various estate agents valued it at what they thought it was worth, but in order to clinch a sale we were obliged to sell at about 20 per cent less than the agents' estimates.

Since then, prices in the same urbanisations have dropped further, particularly if the seller wants or needs a quick sale. Some owners have held out for higher prices encouraged by their estate agent, but some properties have now been on the market for three years leaving the vendor with little choice but to drop the price. Static and dropping prices are a sure sign that there are just too many properties, new and resales, chasing too few buyers. Many potential buyers are now more cautious, worried about the possibility of higher interest rates or a slowing up of property prices in their home country. In addition, the price rises over the last ten years mean that Spanish property is no longer a cheap option for a holiday property. Buyers looking for a cheap deal are increasingly considering Eastern Europe, Turkey or Morocco.

At the time of writing (early 2008), it would appear the bubble has burst – but only for the moment. Prices will rise again, and right now it's a buyer's market. If the vendor is keen to sell it is likely that a reasonable offer will be accepted. Property will always be a good long-term investment.

This could be a good time to buy property in Spain. Prices may drop even lower because there are huge numbers of newly built apartments and townhouses standing empty and unsold. Many of these are owned by property speculators who may have bought several properties off-plan, making staged payments on borrowed money. Their plan was to sell at a profit before they had paid in full for the property. If the banks call in their loans there could be many homes available at very low prices.

'Should I buy a property as an investment?'

If you buy sensibly, now may be a good time to snap up a bargain in Spain. If the vendor needs to sell quickly you could negotiate a good price. If the vendor is an investor who borrowed the money to buy property, you could buy at a very advantageous price.

However, if you plan to buy and resell for a profit in the near future you might want to reconsider. There are many properties which have been on the market for as long as three years.

Buying a holiday property with a view to letting it, is not as profitable as it was in the 1990s because Spain has become more expensive as a holiday destination and there is a huge amount of property available for rent.

Buying as a long-term investment is a safer bet and you would be unlikely to lose out. Where we live, apartments which 20 years ago were on the market for less than £10,000 now sell for over £100,000. However, note the time span.

 'Should I buy a property as a holiday home?'

Buying a holiday home in the right area is one of the best investments you can make, but there are some questions you must ask yourself. Will you be happy to return to the same place time after time, year after year? Many who have already travelled extensively are only too happy to settle on one location.

A holiday home allows you the luxury of having your own possessions around you. It is a bit like having your own private hotel rooms in your chosen location with the added convenience of leaving your holiday clothes in the wardrobe so you can travel light. Remember that if you plan to let the property when you are not there, you will need to have a secure space where you can lock up your personal life. Is there an area which can be made secure?

If you want to let your property, is it attractive to potential clients? This is when location becomes very important. How close are the facilities which the tenant might want, such as shops, restaurants, nightlife, tourist attractions? Would your chosen property appeal to others and not just to you?

Holiday homes in the countryside may not always be such a good investment. The season in the inland areas, even 30 kilometres from the coast, is much shorter. When we were considering a purchase inland I checked out the letting potential with the company who acted as our agents in the UK for our existing property. Their response was that while our coastal apartment was attracting more than 20 weeks rental over a year, most inland properties would struggle to achieve

10 weeks, made up from two- to four-day periods rather than complete weeks – a point worth remembering.

One further important point is that there are currently too many rental properties chasing too few potential clients. The market is not expanding fast enough and many new buyers who want to let their property have been disappointed. If mortgage payments on your new property depend on rental income then you could find yourself facing problems in the future.

However, many estate agents will try to persuade you that there's a good rental market. The relocation TV programmes often tell the potential purchasers the same thing. A typical statement is, 'When you are not here you could earn £500 a week from letting the property, would you be interested in this?' The answer is often yes. The keyword however in this question is 'could'. I have found agents on the Internet who try to say that the properties which they are selling will attract more than 30 weeks rental in a year and produce financial scenarios to illustrate what this could mean in financial returns. At best we have only achieved 24 weeks rental – that is with an agent in the UK and a personal marketing drive through the Internet and through friends. Take these agents' illustrations with a very large pinch of salt and always ask them to prove this kind of occupancy rate.

 ## 'Should I buy a property to live in?'

The BBC survey mentioned earlier suggests that almost a million Brits live in Spain permanently or for a large part of the year. There are however many others whose principal address remains in Britain and who own a holiday home in Spain in which they spend more than six months a year, yet still remain officially British residents. In legal terms, if anyone spends more than six months in Spain, they become tax residents and should pay their taxes in Spain. In practice, many Brits do retain an address in the UK.

In the first urbanisation we lived in, there were 60 apartments and about 50 of them had British owners although less than 20 per cent of those were officially resident in Spain. Multiply this figure by the number of urbanisations the length of the Spanish coastline and you would probably find that the true number of Brits owning property in Spain and living there for most of the year would be closer to two million.

If you decide to move to Spain permanently, rather than just buy a holiday home, it's important that you explore your motivation for doing so beforehand. If Spain holds a fascination because you have had wonderful holidays, think carefully about how it will compare as a permanent country of residence. Building a new life for you and your family in a new country is no easy feat and the decision to do so should not be taken lightly. Make sure you've thought long and hard about the various lifestyle changes involved in a move to Spain, and that you're not looking at everything through rose-tinted spectacles. The following questions will help you with this:

'How easy will it be to find work in Spain?'

If you are below retirement age and need to work to live and pay the bills, it may be difficult to find legitimate work if you don't speak Spanish, even in the coastal areas. You may find seasonal work in English restaurants and bars, but payment is often in cash, which usually means your employer hasn't registered you with the labour authorities and you have no employee rights.

Compared to some other EU countries, unemployment rates in Spain are fairly high (over 10 per cent in some areas) and any available jobs will usually go to a Spaniard. There is a real need to be able to speak fluent Spanish if you are going to find work with a local employer, even in coastal areas.

However, there are many British expats who are making a very good living in Spain by offering services to their fellow countrymen. English-speaking electricians, plumbers, decorators, builders, and motor mechanics can all be found in the coastal areas. You can usually find them by word-of-mouth recommendation or from adverts in the English-language newspapers. Many are running unregistered businesses (officially illegal) and they may not be paying their Spanish social security charges because they are working for cash. Without paying the social security payments, they are not entitled to medical cover, unemployment benefit or Spanish pensions in the future.

Should you decide to follow your trade in Spain and offer services to English-speaking clients – and there is a good market for this in the coastal areas – you really should make yourself legal. Register yourself as a builder or plumber and sign up to pay social security and *IVA* (Spanish VAT) so that you can offer your clients VAT invoices, which may help them with future Capital Gains Tax issues. It isn't difficult to register especially with the help of a *gestor* (an agent who will help you with bureaucracy) and the earnings you can make without paying business taxes are very generous. You will have to pay Spanish social security charges which are around €250 minimum per month but this will mean that you are contributing to a Spanish pension and to state healthcare. Working the 'black' (cash) economy does not actually benefit you or your clients in the long term. Use this fact as part of your marketing tactics when attracting clients.

To set yourself up properly you would be advised to use the services of a *gestor*, who isn't a lawyer or financial adviser, but works alongside them, battling through Spanish bureaucracy on your behalf. The role of the *gestor* is explained in full in Chapter 7.

Many people who have moved to Spain end up working in bars or restaurants. They are often paid cash in hand with no social security charges deducted and no contract of employment. Officially they don't exist in the eyes of the state and the employer can terminate their employment for any reason without notice because they will face no legal repercussions. However, there are frequent inspections, especially during the summer months, and employers who are illegally employing workers can be heavily fined.

There are many other Brits who have found legitimate work with estate agents and who are paying social security charges but such work tends to be very strongly commission-based and very unpredictable, particularly in the current market downturn.

Don't forget that under EU rules if you live in an EU country for more than six months a year that is where you pay tax, usually on your worldwide income – consult your *gestor*. There are many foreigners in Spain who are not paying income tax in any EU country, managing to avoid the taxman both in Spain and their home country. However, as the EU tightens up on the rules and the tax authorities in both countries exchange information, it's unlikely that many people will slip through the net.

In south-western Andalusia there are many British residents who have found work in Gibraltar. Obviously English is the language of business there and if you find work you will have to contribute to the social security system in Gibraltar. If it's a permanent job you will be expected to pay towards a Gibraltarian pension and local healthcare with a doctor or hospital treatment. Employment in Gibraltar will not entitle you to any healthcare in Spain.

Many others have set up legitimate businesses, such as bars, guesthouses, restaurants, bookshops, florists, hairdressers, and even computer businesses because many expats need their English computers. In the right area these businesses can do very well, but it's very important to do market research and find out if there is a need locally for the kind of services you are offering and before you make the decision to relocate.

If you have professional qualifications it is possible to have these recognised in Spain under EU directives and maybe open the door to a new business venture. For example, most of the vets we encountered in Spain were of Dutch or German origin. However, getting your qualification recognised by the Spanish authorities can be a long and complicated business, and depends on how your profession is regulated or whether it's recognised in Spain. The Spanish Embassy can advise you and start the process before you leave the UK, or you can contact the National Academic Recognition Information Centre (NARIC) www.naric.org.uk, who should be able to help. If you're thinking of running a business which depends on professional qualifications, it will be far easier if you can speak Spanish because you may have, or want to attract, Spanish clients as well as expats.

Most of these job opportunities are available in the coastal areas where there is a large expat population who speak little or no Spanish and want to deal with English-speaking suppliers.

If your dream is to live and work in rural Spain then you really will need to speak Spanish.

There are many younger British residents who are also looking for a better lifestyle for themselves and their family, and Spain could also be their ideal destination. However, if you move to Spain with your family to provide them with a better quality of life, you need to be prepared for all kinds of situations. Finding employment – or setting up a business which means that you contribute to Spanish social security payments – is the best way to put your mind at rest. That way you and your family can use the Spanish healthcare system and, if you pay enough contributions before retire, you will be able to claim a pension. Unless you have worked for 30 years or more in the UK you will not get a full UK state pension. In Spain, you must have contributed for at least 15 years to receive a state pension, but if you contribute nothing, the state provides nothing when you retire.

If you are retired and have an income, you do not need to worry about the availability of work locally, and you can have your UK state pension paid directly into your Spanish bank account. More importantly, you do not need to worry about any contributions to Spanish social security. If you've reached retirement age and have paid social security contributions in the UK, you're entitled to free healthcare in Spain under EU legislation, although you must present form E121 to the health authorities in Spain. The form can be obtained from the Department for Work and Pensions in the UK.

'Is my partner or family as committed to this dream as me?'

If you are in a relationship, both partners (and more importantly, if there is a family involved, your children) must be in total agreement that relocation is the right move before any irrevocable decision is taken. I say irrevocable because once you have stepped off the UK property ladder it can be difficult, if not impossible, to return to where you came from. For example, the house we left in south-west London has appreciated in value by £200,000 since we left six years ago but our Spanish property has not increased by the same proportion, and we certainly could not afford to return to that house.

Other people may have enjoyed a very metropolitan lifestyle in the UK and they may find it difficult to adjust to the fact that their new life is very different. This is especially true if they choose to live a long way from built-up areas, and it can lead to potential conflict within the family. There might be fewer restaurants and shops; more limited access to the arts such as the theatre and the cinema. There is plenty of culture around, but usually the language is Spanish; finding English theatre in Spain is very difficult, if not impossible.

On occasions, children can have difficulty fitting in to a new school, particularly if their new education is in a foreign language. Of course, children's problems usually become problems for their parents, and unhappy children are not conducive to a happy relationship between the parents. Relationships can be even more strained if one member of the partnership finds work in Spain, and the other partner has to remain at home to look after the children with little command of the language and few local friends.

'How does the Spanish education system differ from the UK system?'

Education is compulsory in Spain from 6–16 years. State education is free, but in most provinces parents have to buy their children's books and materials for arts and crafts classes – this costs around €125 every year. The main difference between the Spanish and British education systems is that, in Spain, schools teach in a very formal way with the students sitting at desks set up in rows rather than around large tables and pupils tend to learn information by rote. School uniforms are not normally worn in Spanish state schools, but they are in the private sector.

Children from birth to six years can take advantage of what's called *educación infantil* (infant education), which is optional and free to all. *Educación infantil* is in two separate phases; from birth to three years, when they attend a type of kindergarten and from three to six years, when children attend nursery school and are prepared for primary school. Most Spanish parents now regard this second stage as an integral part of their child's education and many primary schools now have *infantil* classes.

At the age of six every child must move on to the next phase, known as *educación primaria* (primary school). This is organised into three cycles of two years. At the end of each cycle failure to pass all the examinations could result in the student being asked to repeat a year, although this system is currently under review. The times of the primary school day vary according to where you live. They could be 9 a.m. to 12.30 p.m. and 3.30 p.m. to 5 p.m. or 9 a.m. to 2 p.m. during the hot weather. The Spanish government is trying to set a regular time in primary schools. Secondary schools generally operate a school day which starts at 8.15 a.m. and finishes at 2.30 p.m. School holidays are broadly similar to those in the UK but with shorter holidays at Christmas and Easter and a longer summer holiday. The curriculum is rather like the UK curriculum several decades ago with an emphasis on the more traditional skills of reading, writing and arithmetic.

The next compulsory stage in education is *educación secundaria obligatoria* (secondary education, known as *ESO*) which takes the student from 12–16 years. Secondary schools try to identify whether the student should follow vocational training (offered in the school), or an academic training. At the end of this period and having passed the examinations the student will be awarded the title of *graduado/a de educación secundaria obligatoria* (graduate of secondary education) which will allow them to do one of three things:

- Enter into full time vocational training at a technical college.
- Continue in school for another two years, studying for the *Bachillerato*, a qualification similar to A Level studies in the UK, which will allow the student to sit university entrance exams or proceed to a higher level college for vocational training such as computer sciences, management studies or engineering.
- Join the world of the employed.

There's no shortage of schools in Spain and virtually every village of any size will have a primary school and most large towns have a secondary school. School buses are an important part of Spanish school life, both at primary and secondary level, and the school run as carried out by many parents in the UK does not happen in Spain.

After school there are many good universities in Spain and if your children leave school with the right qualifications they can gain entrance to Spanish universities or indeed universities around the world, (although many UK citizens, resident in

Spain, do send their children back to the UK for university or further education). For those registered as foreign residents, bursaries are available to support university education in Spain according to the income of the parents.

'As non-native Spanish speakers how will my children fare at school?'

This will depend on where you choose to live and much money you have at your disposal. If you live in the coastal areas and can afford the international schools, your children will receive a similar education to that in the UK. If you live in the inland areas where all education is in Spanish, your children could have more problems, but all indications are that children pick up the language very quickly, although this does depend on their age and enthusiasm for life in Spain.

In the big cities and in many of the coastal areas there are international schools at both primary and secondary level. In these schools, teaching is in English and usually follows the UK curriculum, your children will also be educated alongside many other nationalities. They will be guided through a programme of education which will take them towards either GCSEs and A Levels or the International Baccalaureate, both of which are recognised by universities around the world as an entrance qualification. However, international schools are private schools and the fees can be high.

If you choose to live in an area where access to international schools is difficult (or you can't afford private education), then your children will have to attend a local Spanish state school where they will be educated in Spanish under the excellent Spanish educational system. Some schools in the coastal areas offer additional tuition in Spanish for non-Spanish speakers, although in inland areas this rarely happens.

This is not as worrying as it sounds because children under ten tend to pick up languages very quickly. You will soon find that your children are bilingual, and will probably end up helping you with your Spanish. Older children usually take longer to pick up the language and adapt.

We have friends who have enrolled their children in Spanish schools and have experienced very few problems. Occasionally, there may be a little resentment from Spanish parents about increased class sizes because of non-Spanish children attending the local school. However, this generally becomes less of a problem as you and your children integrate and make some Spanish friends.

The problem of crowded class sizes could be overcome if every expat registered themselves with their local authority in Spain. Spanish authorities provide local services according to the official size of the local population. If, for example, the local population is officially 200,000, then schools, post offices, police, fire services and all the other local facilities will be based on this figure. If however, the local population is actually 300,000 then the services will naturally be lacking.

'What should I know about healthcare?'

In very simple terms, if you have not contributed to the Spanish healthcare system you will not be entitled to state healthcare unless you are a retired EU citizen. In this situation your country of origin funds your healthcare under EU reciprocal agreements. However, you must register form E121 with the Spanish health authorities.

When you leave the UK, you can take an E106 form which is available from the Department for Work and Pensions. This will provide healthcare cover for up to two years, but you will only be entitled to an E106 if you have been paying National Insurance right up to the day you leave the UK. The E106 also gives you time to shop around for private healthcare or to find a job and begin paying Spanish social security contributions.

If you leave the UK to live permanently in Spain (or indeed any other destination) and you no longer have a registered British address, you are no longer entitled to NHS treatment and you should surrender your NHS card as you leave the country. Should you fall ill, you can't just jump on a plane and return to the UK in order to go to a GP or hospital. I discovered this when I contacted my former NHS surgery in London while researching an earlier book and had to admit that I now lived permanently in Spain. I was informed that my name would be deleted from the list and that my medical records would be sent to a central file. My medical records belonged to the state and not to me. Should you return to live permanently in the UK, you can of course re-register.

One important factor which must be taken into account if you are retired and decide to live in Spain, is that there is a great lack of retirement or care homes should you need care in the future. It is the custom in Spain that the family look after elderly relatives – not the state. Even in hospitals, the family often help to provide nursing care to the patients. This is not a real problem for the local population who often have an extended family, but it could be a serious problem for elderly expats, especially when one partner dies. You should also remember that there are very few English-speaking staff in state hospitals (even in coastal areas) which could cause problems if you do not speak Spanish. Some have voluntary interpreters, but they are often not available when you need them.

In the past, many Brits in Spain have depended on the old E111 form which has now been replaced by the European Health Insurance Card (EHIC). This is available from the Post Office or online, but is only intended to provide emergency healthcare for EU citizens while on holiday in another EU country. It should not be used to cover permanent healthcare provision for a British citizen who actually lives in Spain. If you're discovered using it in this way, you will be charged for your healthcare.

If you pay Spanish social security charges you will qualify for state healthcare, but if you work for cash without a contract of employment you will not qualify so you must budget for private healthcare. UK private healthcare is very expensive, but in Spain charges are reasonable and cover GP consultations and hospital care. My partner and I, in our late fifties and early sixties, pay the equivalent of £110 per month in total for GP and hospital care. Prescriptions, dental treatment and optical treatment are not covered although one visit a year to a dental hygienist is covered.

The real difference we have found is that when you visit a private GP the consultation is as long as it needs to be, and in the public sector waiting times are similar to those in the UK. In the private sector, you will not encounter any 10 minute maximum consultation time, because if your doctor does not offer you a good service you are perfectly entitled to consult another doctor the next time. A private consultation with a GP costs less than €30 and we know many people who consult a GP privately and then fall back on the Spanish equivalent of the NHS for hospital care if they are registered to receive it. Private and state healthcare exist side-by-side in Spain so you are entitled to consult a GP privately and then go to hospital under the state system.

In addition, if any tests are carried out you will be given a copy of the results for your personal file – whereas in the UK your test results belong to the NHS and remain with the NHS even when you leave the country. If you have a complicated medical history this could cause problems, although you can request and pay for a summary of your medical records which you can then present to your Spanish GP.

State GP care in Spain is good although waiting times are longer than with private GPs. There are many English-speaking GPs in private medicine, but most of these are primarily based in the big cities or in the coastal areas. In remote country areas English-speaking doctors are virtually impossible to find because the majority, if not all, of their patients are local Spaniards who are part of the state system.

Overall, the quality of healthcare in Spain is far superior to that in the UK. Hospitals are impressive although those offering specialist care tend to be a fair distance from one another, so if you don't live close to a major centre, hospital care or hospital visiting may mean a lot of travelling.

'What should I know about other public services?'

In the coastal areas public transport services are very good, with regular and inexpensive bus services (usually in air-conditioned coaches) serving the local area (although journey times can be quite long because the bus calls at all the local towns on the way). The rail network around the coast is good in most areas and is currently being extended. For example, the high speed rail connection from Madrid (known as the *AVE*) has been extended to Malaga with a journey time of just 2.5 hours and will eventually reach Estepona and beyond.

Although household services in Spain have been officially privatised for several years now, in practice, they operate near monopolies and there is not the same opportunity you would have in the UK to choose an alternative supplier of electricity or water. Mains gas is only available in the large cities, so in many areas consumers have to rely on bottled gas which is not expensive. Telephone and internet services are dominated by *Telefónica*, the former state-owned company, which was privatised in 1997. You can sign up for cheaper telephone calls from other companies who have pre-pay telephone services. In developed areas, broadband Internet connection is available but in remote country areas it's unlikely that you will have Internet access and you may be forced to rely on a satellite connection.

'Will I need to speak Spanish?'

If you move to the coastal resort areas the answer to this can be both yes and no! The reason for this is that it depends on where you live and whether you choose to integrate with Spaniards or not. Even in expat areas where English is widely spoken, an ability to get by in Spanish is a definite advantage – and it's only polite to at least try to speak to Spaniards in their own language. However, while researching this book I discovered that less than 10 per cent of the expat population in the coastal areas have any knowledge of Spanish.

Your ability, desire or intention to learn Spanish could be a very important factor in your final choice of location for a property in Spain. If you decide to move to a major city or a coastal area, many of the local authorities offer tuition in Spanish (although many expats fail to take up this offer because they think they don't need to learn the language).

There's no denying that you can get by with little or no Spanish in some areas but even the basics make your life far more interesting and rewarding. Don't forget you may want to query a bill, communicate with Town Hall officials or more importantly, with a doctor in an emergency. Interpreters never seem to be around when you need them most. If your life runs smoothly, you will be fine, but when it doesn't, it's a major bonus to be able to communicate for yourself rather than rely on others.

In many of the coastal areas you will often be hard-pressed to hear a Spanish voice and instead you will find yourself surrounded by English, German or Scandinavian voices. As long as you don't move too far from these areas, you could live quite happily for many years without ever having to speak to a local person in Spanish. This is why so few of the new residents try to learn, despite the fact that it means they don't get to venture far or discover more about their adopted country. Remember that there will be occasions when you need to deal with bureaucracy and local government officials will rarely speak English to you. In these situations you can always ask a friend to go along with you as a translator or pay someone to sort it out for you. In some popular coastal areas, the Town Hall has a Foreigner's Department, where staff will help you in many different languages.

Perhaps the reason that there's such a large English population in Spain is the appeal of not having to learn a new language. Some think that if they need to speak Spanish they can just add 'io' to the English words they are using. I will never forget the English President of our urbanisation telling the Spanish gardeners that today 'you must cuttio the grassio'. I also remember one of my first attempts at Spanish; we had just moved there and I had completed a course of intensive Spanish lessons, I went into a bar and ordered in Spanish only to have the waiter reply, 'Would you mind ordering again in English?' in a very strong Irish accent!

If you decide to move even a few kilometres inland from the coasts and certainly if you plan to go to almost any other part of Spain, you must be able to speak the language if you want to integrate and be accepted by the local population. Spaniards love it if you try to speak their language and are always happy to help and encourage you. In much of Spain you don't get a choice about which language you speak, it's Spanish or nothing but the benefit of this is that you learn very quickly! Don't despair; Spanish is not a difficult language to learn - especially if you already have a knowledge of French or Latin. Remember that if you move to Catalonia, which includes Barcelona and the Costa Brava, you should have a good working knowledge of the Catalan language and a fairly good grasp of Castilian Spanish.

At the end of later chapters I have provided a glossary of words or terms which could be useful for readers.

'How does the climate change throughout the year?'

Many people who buy property in Spain do so because the climate appears to be ideal; their experiences of the Spanish climate are based on holidays in the sun when it was perhaps raining at home. What they enjoyed was two weeks in the sun with virtually no prospect of rain and they naturally think that it's a wonderful place to live!

Depending on where you choose to settle, you should be prepared for blisteringly hot summers, particularly throughout July and August when there is very little respite from the heat because even the nights can be very warm. In the coastal areas around the Mediterranean this is normal and you will enjoy possibly more than 300 days of sunshine a year.

However, on the days when the sun does not shine there can be torrential rain which might even stop you going outside. Winter evenings can also be decidedly chilly, which is why so many Spanish properties have log burning stoves – they are necessary and are not just for decoration. Many other homeowners are installing air-conditioning although personally I prefer good old-fashioned ceiling fans. What is the point of living in a warm climate if you have to keep the doors closed all day so that the air-conditioning works properly?

Only a few miles inland from the Costa del Sol, the Sierra Nevada is an important winter sports area with major snowfalls in the winter months. This is wonderful for many local inhabitants because they can have winter sports holidays without having to travel long distances. Many new residents are often surprised that it snows so heavily a few kilometres inland from the Mediterranean.

Brits moving to Spain need to adjust to the lack of recognisable seasons as they have known them. Palm trees are a constant all year round – throughout the very hot summers and the warm and sometimes wet winters. Wild flowers bloom in October following the first rain after the hot and arid summer but you won't experience the traditional arrival of spring with daffodils and all the other spring flowers. There are very few deciduous trees in the coastal areas and even inland from the Mediterranean a lot of the trees are pines so there are no autumn leaves to admire (or rake up off your garden path).

As you move towards northern Spain and areas such as Asturias, Galicia and Cantabria, known as 'Green Spain', recognisable seasons appear again as the climate is far wetter and the coast is influenced by the Atlantic. Central Spain is on a very high plateau, known as the *Meseta,* which is very dry with hot summers and potentially very cold winters. Madrid for example can be much colder than the UK in the height of the winter. Madrid is actually the highest capital city in Europe in terms of height above sea level.

If you dream of a life in the sun, consider the climate carefully in the area of Spain you're interested in, but also think about the realities of year-round sunshine before you make any decisions.

'What relationships will I have with family and friends back in the UK?'

Not only is it essential that your partner and family are 100 per cent behind your decision to move abroad, you also might need to consider the relatives and friends you're leaving behind.

In an ideal world your loved ones would be happy to see you achieve your dream of a new life in Spain, but in reality they often resent the fact that you have moved abroad. During my expat experiences I have known grandparents who have followed their children to the new destination and I have also known expat grandparents who love their life in the sun but just cannot cope without seeing their grandchildren grow up on a day-to-day basis. Often the grandmother wants to be back in the UK to see the new baby grow, while grandfather wants to stay in Spain – these situations can cause great tension in family relationships. I have also seen examples of couples who have children and resent the fact that Grandma has moved to Spain and is no longer there to be an unpaid child minder.

Then we come to the question of friends. Friends from home can be divided into two distinct categories: the first are those who say, 'We must never lose touch' and, 'I'll miss you so much' when you leave, but two weeks later they seem to have forgotten that you ever existed, the second are the true friends who may be very few, but who do keep in touch and I am very happy that I still have friends whom I have known 30 years who still come to stay, but I must admit they are in the minority. The most important point is that in your new life you will make many new friends of all different kinds, other expats, Spaniards and people of all nationalities.

The other thing which can happen is that once you begin your new life you suddenly develop new best friends. These are the ones who see the possibility of a free holiday and if you're not careful you can find yourself running free bed and breakfast accommodation where you do the airport run, and act as the local tour guide to take your visitors to all the local sights which you have seen on numerous occasions. Although your guests might take you out for a few meals at their expense, you end up spending a huge amount of money eating out and day-tripping which you would not normally have done.

Guests, unless they are very close family or friends must be encouraged to rent a car and find their own way to your property. With a car they can be independent and the breakfast conversation will then be 'What are you going to do today?' rather than the guests saying 'What are we going to do today?' Sometimes it is a great relief when these 'new best friends' actually go out for the day and leave you to your own life.

'If we decide to live in Spain, what should we do with our house in the UK?'

If you sell in the UK, you will be stepping off the UK property ladder and it could be very difficult to get back onto it should you ultimately decide that you might have made a mistake.

In our case there was no option because there was no way that we could have maintained a house in London with all the expenses involved and afford to buy a house in Spain. We needed the capital appreciation on the UK property to fund the purchase in Spain and to provide additional investment income for our new life.

Friends said to us 'Why don't you let the London property? The income will help you to buy in Spain.' They had a point, but absentee landlords can have real problems. The London house would have had to be put into the hands of a letting agent who would have taken a healthy commission from the rent achieved - perhaps as much as 20 per cent. By the time the government took their share of the rent (in the form of income tax) we would probably just have covered the tail end of the mortgage we had on the house. We knew the house next door to us in London was a rental investment (for long-term rentals), and every time a tenant left the owner had to completely re-decorate before a new tenant could be found. This would be a further drain on the rental income even if the cost of re-decoration was tax deductible.

In the end, there is no substitute for being bold and cashing in your chips and relocating to a new property which you can buy outright with no mortgage. If you're lucky enough to be able to do this all you need for the future is enough income to pay the utility bills and buy food.

The only compromise on this front, which I do recommend, is to let your UK property for a year while you rent in Spain to determine whether or not you're happy with the decision to relocate. If you do this you can always return 'home' having lost nothing. Also, if you rent first in Spain you will be absolutely certain that your chosen location is where you want to live and you will have the luxury of viewing properties on a more leisurely basis than on a rushed inspection trip.

 Summary

- **Why do I want to buy a property in Spain?**
- **Do I want to buy property purely as an investment?**
- **Do I want to live there permanently or do I want a holiday home?**
- **Will I find work if I need an income?**
- **Does my family want to move as much as I do?**
- **How will my children get on at school?**
- **Have I checked out healthcare and can I afford private healthcare?**
- **Do I need or want to learn the language?**
- **Will I cope with the climate?**
- **How will my family and friends back home react to the move?**
- **Will I be accepted by the locals?**
- **What should I do with my present property?**

Chapter 2

Where should I look for a property in Spain?

Spain is the third largest country in Europe with a population of 40.5 million (2007 estimate). A large percentage of the population (77 per cent) is based in urban or coastal areas, which account for less than 10 per cent of the land mass, and the remaining 23 per cent live in rural areas. The coastal areas around the Mediterranean and the big cities; Madrid, Barcelona, Valencia, Seville and Zaragoza are quite highly populated and can be very busy, particularly in the summer months at the height of the tourist season, while inland areas can appear to be almost deserted and indeed, many are.

Wherever you go in Spain during the summer months you will usually find sun, but some parts of the country can be decidedly different during the winter months, with violent thunderstorms and torrential rain. The north of Spain has a climate which resembles Cornwall in the UK, so the temperature in the summer is very bearable and the land green and pleasant.

 ### 'With such a large area to consider, where do you start looking?'

Many Brits end up buying in an area where they have enjoyed regular holidays because they feel they know that region and feel comfortable there. Indeed many of our friends in Spain only know the area in which they now live because they spent many holidays there before taking the step to move to the region, and many decided to buy a property while on holiday.

This is not a mistake and certainly makes good sense if you're looking for a holiday property, but the perfect holiday home and in an ideal holiday area may not be the best choice for a permanent home. In the traditional tourist areas many visitors do not venture more than ten miles inland from the coast so they may think they know the area, but they could be just a few miles from their dream destination without even knowing it. This is one reason why it's a good idea to rent first and thoroughly investigate the local area.

Friends who rented in our urbanisation did exactly that, they moved from the UK with a view to living permanently in Spain and rented an apartment. The husband was a skilled motor mechanic who specialised in classic British cars. He had very few problems finding work because there was a local need for his skills, but he wanted to do more than just work for someone else. Within 18 months they had sold their UK property and found a house which they loved in a village 5 kilometres inland and he had set himself up in business in the same village. However, he had done his market research and realised that close to the village was one of the most affluent areas in the Costa del Sol where many residents drive classic British cars. Even better, there was no competition to his business. This is a great success story which others can also achieve with the right amount of hard work, research and determination.

What follows is an analysis of various popular areas in Spain, entering through its north-eastern border with France and beginning with the Costa Brava.

 ## 'What should I know about the Costa Brava?'

The area just south of the border with France, the province of Catalonia (population 6.8 million), is home to one of the most beautiful coastal areas in Spain. Here you are still in the foothills of the Pyrenees and the mountains tumble down into the Mediterranean.

In the northern part of this region the coastal areas have many beautiful villages and small towns and, because of the mountainous terrain, there is far less development than you find further south. There is almost nowhere to build on this northern coast since in many areas the mountains literally drop into the sea. Catalonia also has very strict laws on development (this of course means that property prices are higher). Inland there are wonderful small cities like Girona, a medieval masterpiece, and many beautiful stone-built small towns. There are also many stone-built country properties but many still do not have modern facilities although these could be added. The real Costa Brava ends at Barcelona, which is one of Europe's most fascinating and beautiful cities – a city which was transformed for the

Olympics in 1992. Property prices in Barcelona are very high but if you love cities and can afford the prices, it's a wonderful environment to live in.

Property prices are relatively high across the entire region because there's easy access to both Girona and Barcelona airports, and Montpellier and Perpignan airports in France. Hence there's a wide range of scheduled and charter services to worldwide destinations. In addition, there are excellent motorway and railway connections with the rest of Europe. This is one area of Spain where driving from the UK is a relatively easy option.

One thing that should be considered about this region is that in Catalonia, certainly north of Barcelona, a good knowledge of Spanish is vital, particularly if you're considering a permanent home. Most of the population is bilingual but they speak Catalan first, Castilian Spanish second and very few people speak English. Even finding a taxi driver in Barcelona who speaks English can be a problem.

The climate on the Costa Brava is Mediterranean, although the proximity of the mountains does mean that there is more rain than you might expect and thunderstorms are frequent. I once rented a villa on the northern Costa Brava which was high in the hills behind the sea with a wonderful view of the Bay of Rosas. On several occasions I was actually above a thunderstorm which had rolled down from the Pyrenees. In the height of the summer there can be thunderstorms virtually every day. Winters can be cool and if you move inland winters can be very cold indeed with a lot of snow, although a bonus is that you're within easy reach of the winter sports facilities of the Pyrenees.

'What should I know about the Costa Dorada?'

South of Barcelona is an area known as the Costa Dorada which is still part of Catalonia. This is home to some of the less attractive holiday resorts dating back to the early days of package holidays, although there are still some very beautiful coastal towns in the region. The land is less mountainous here and so more development is taking place although it's not as extensive as it is further south. Development here is still controlled by the Catalonian Government.

Further south the land flattens out even more as you approach the delta of the Ebro River, which is a protected natural park and one of Europe's top birdwatching areas. Prices in this region are, on average, higher than those in the more southerly parts of the country because communications with the rest of Europe by road, rail or air are excellent.

The climate on both the Costa Brava and the Costa Dorada is very good but winters can be cooler than some of the other Costas.

 ## *'What should I know about the Costa Blanca?'*

Moving south brings us to the province of Valencia (population 4.5 million), the Costa del Azahar (Orange Blossom Coast) and the Costa Blanca which is a little further south. The Costa Blanca is home to the famous package holiday resort towns, such as Calpe, Dénia, Jávea and of course the 'Manhattan' of Spain, Benidorm, because of the huge number of high rise buildings in the town. Unfortunately that is where the comparison ends, although many visitors love it and return year after year. Communications with the rest of Spain are good and there are airports at Valencia and Alicante which, although not international hubs, have good scheduled, charter and budget airline services to many airports in the UK.

The coastal areas are very over-developed, yet building continues and properties still sell. The Costa Blanca features heavily in British property exhibitions and could be a paradise for many potential expats, especially if you like the idea of being surrounded by your fellow countrymen. Building density is quite high but that is what helps to keep the prices at an affordable level, although personally this doesn't appeal to me. If you're looking for a Spanish golfing paradise, the Costa Blanca isn't for you as there are fewer courses in this region than in other coastal areas.

Behind this coast the land is flat and there are acres of orange groves – the citrus harvest is important for the local economy, second only to tourism. Behind the orange groves are hills and mountains and an intrepid house-hunter could find some amazing property in some of the hill villages and still enjoy good access to the rest of the world through the coastal towns.

Although there is a lot of development on this coast, the region has a lot to offer from a lifestyle point of view. The climate is Mediterranean with long hot summers and very mild winters. This area is within the Valencian community which has received a lot of negative publicity about what's known as the 'Valencia land grab' law, which you should be aware of and which I will explain later in the book.

 ## 'What should I know about the Costa Cálida?'

This is a new Costa which has only emerged in the last few years. Up until about ten years ago, visitors to Spain jumped from the Costa Blanca to the Costa del Sol and ignored the south-east corner of Spain centred around the region of Murcia which remains relatively under-populated (population 1.3 million). The Costa Cálida, which means the warm coast, has a typical Mediterranean climate with long hot summers and mild winters. It has always been a very important agricultural area but its place on the tourist map is a relatively recent development. The region does have a wonderful coastline which includes the famous Mar Menor, the largest salt water lake in Europe, well-known for its water sports and the exclusive La Manga golf resort.

Communications with the rest of Spain and Europe remain relatively poor, although they are being developed and this is fast becoming one of Spain's property 'hotspots'. For the moment, it is much cheaper than the Costa Blanca or the Costa del Sol.

The major tourist destination in the region is La Manga, which is mentioned above. It's a complex of golf courses and expensive, upmarket living accommodation which has been very successful and now other coastal areas are being similarly developed. Property prices remain very competitive at the moment and for anyone contemplating relocation to Spain, the Costa Cálida could be a really interesting proposition, although it might be quite a few years before it rivals the existing Costas, which may be a good thing for many people. The current, relatively low levels of development could increase dramatically and this coast may eventually look like the other Costas.

There are no major airports in the region but some of the holiday charters and budget airlines fly into Almeria and Murcia.

 ### 'What should I know about Andalusia?'

Andalusia is a vast region which consists of eight provinces. Here you will find the Costa Tropical, the Costa del Sol and the Costa de la Luz together with a vast inland region, some of which is developed but some of which remains very wild.

Andalusia is the second largest region of Spain and the most populated (population 7.7 million) and for many it encapsulates the entire country in one region. This is truly the Spain of the classic guide book; centuries of Moorish occupation, bullfighting, flamenco and the brash coastal resorts of the Costa del Sol, the sun, sea and sangria of Torremolinos and Fuengirola, the international chic of Marbella and Puerto Banús and everything in between.

Up until the 1960s, it was one of the poorest regions in Spain. Mass tourism and rampant development began in the 1960s and building has hardly stopped since. Very few properties, apart from village houses or remote country properties, are more than 40 years old.

My partner visited Torremolinos on holiday in the early 1960s when mass tourism was just starting and at that time the town was still just a fishing village with a few new hotels. The road from Torremolinos to Gibraltar (to which access was denied by General Franco) was not much more than a dirt track at some points, Marbella as it is now did not exist, and all along the coast all you could see were small fishing villages with the boats drawn up on the beach. The ferry to Tangier from Algeciras was little more than an ancient wooden vessel filled with people and animals being ferried from Europe to Africa and vice-versa.

Contrast that with the Costa del Sol of today with its high-rise properties, manicured gardens, marinas, golf courses, motorways and dual carriageways, and hydrofoils transporting tourists from Spain to Morocco on day trips to the souks – so much development in 40 years and still it continues.

This is one area where there is a glut of resale properties built 20-30 years ago, and an even bigger glut of brand new properties built during the last few years in an attempt to take advantage of a booming world property market. With so many properties chasing a diminishing number of buyers this could be a very good time for someone who wants to move to Spain permanently or buy a holiday home at a good price, or make an offer on a property which the vendor is desperate to shift.

The Costa del Sol is very developed and the western end between Estepona and Gibraltar (which was largely undeveloped during the 1990s) has now seen a huge explosion in new build property partly because of better motorway access in recent years. In addition, the coast road has been improved making access to Malaga and Gibraltar airports easier than ever.

The one part of the Andalusian coast which remains relatively undeveloped is the Costa de la Luz, on the Atlantic coast between Gibraltar and Portugal. It remains very Spanish and there aren't, for the moment anyway, a huge amount of new build properties. The Atlantic influence means that it's cooler in the summer and colder and windier in the winter. In fact it is windy all year round which has resulted in one of the resorts, Tarifa, becoming the windsurfing capital of Europe. The major city on this coast is Cádiz and access by air is probably easier through Seville or Jerez airports rather than Malaga.

There are still plenty of interesting villages where property is available but it is far more Spanish than the Costa del Sol and if you're interested in this area, it's important to be able to speak Spanish.

The final part of this coast before you reach the Portuguese border is a huge nature reserve, the Cota Doñana National

Park. There are very few properties for sale in the surrounding areas and if you can find one you will really be in rural Spain.

Communication with the rest of Europe from this region is good via Malaga airport, although it can be very busy during the summer months with long delays. However, Malaga is the main international airport on the Costa del Sol and is currently undergoing major expansion and it will eventually have a new terminal building. The Spanish equivalent of the high speed train (*Alta Velocidad Española,* known simply as the *AVE*) has also been extended to reach Malaga. There are excellent motorway systems along the coast and a good motorway from Malaga to Madrid. The western end of the coast has air connections through Gibraltar airport although there are not many daily flights and these are mainly to the UK. This will change now that Iberia, the Spanish national airline has been given permission to fly to Gibraltar. Road connections from the western end of the Costa del Sol or the Costa de la Luz are good with motorways going via Seville.

Andalusia is also known for its wonderful unspoilt inland areas where mass tourism has hardly had an effect. It's home to some beautiful cities and towns where history has left an amazing legacy in places like Malaga, Granada, Córdoba, Jaén, Ronda, Jerez, Cádiz and Seville. During your drive around these larger towns and cities you will encounter smaller towns, many classified as *pueblos blancos* such as Antequera, Competa, Coin, Alhaurin, Mijas, Benahavís, Ojén, Casares, Gaucín and Jimena de la Frontera. Many of these villages and towns have already been colonised by expat buyers and really good restored village houses can now be quite expensive although some un-restored property still exists. The influx of new foreign residents has changed the face of many of the villages, leaving them with a far less Spanish feel.

There is one area which is relatively undeveloped to the north-east of Malaga and within the provinces of Granada and Almeria and that is the mountainous region, known as *Las Alpujarras*. However, even in this region property prices have risen since the publication of several best-selling books describing a return to nature in this region. Further north into the hinterland of Andalusia there are still real property bargains to be found but the further you go from the coast and the further you rise into the Sierra Nevada, the more careful you will have to be about what you buy. This is a relatively unspoilt and undeveloped area and there may still be a considerable number of illegally built properties, a topic which I will explore in more detail in Chapter 5.

Inland, the summer can be viciously hot but conversely winters can be bitterly cold with dramatic snowfalls. Seville is considered to be one of the hottest cities in Europe. Many of the old farmhouses which arrive on the market are very basic with no services apart from well-water. It's sometimes possible to connect to a mains electricity supply, but you should check how close the nearest pylons are and take advice from your lawyer and local electricity authority.

Ease of access should always be checked. It might be difficult but achievable between March and October but could be virtually impossible during the height of the winter without a powerful 4 x 4 vehicle. In addition, it's often impossible to have a landline telephone connection in inland areas. We have friends who only live a few miles inland who have to depend on a satellite telephone or a mobile.

It's important to understand that many of the local Spaniards who live in these remote properties can't understand why they're so appealing to immigrants from northern Europe looking for their Spanish dream. However, they aren't slow to seize the opportunity to sell at the highest possible price to an enthusiastic foreigner and use the proceeds to go and buy a modern apartment on the coast, complete with all mod cons, thereby fulfilling their own personal Spanish dream!

'What should I know about inland Spain?'

Travel only 60 or 70 kilometres inland from any of the coastal regions in Spain and you will find yourself in a totally different environment, what many people call real Spain. This is where, if you are a true pioneer and can speak Spanish, you could really change your life. In truly inland Spain, nestled in the regions of Castile-la Mancha (*Castilla-La Mancha*) in the centre of the country, Extremadura, in the far west of Spain and further north, Castile and León (*Castilla y León*) - the total population of all three regions is only around 5 million - you could be many kilometres from your nearest neighbour. You could also find yourself a long way from the nearest town with good services and amenities, such as doctors, a pharmacy, a supermarket, a school or a hospital and even further from a railway station. Your nearest airport is Madrid which could be around 200 kilometres away.

Inland property prices can seem very inexpensive compared with those in coastal regions. You will need to visit your chosen region and find out what properties are for sale because this area doesn't have the same kind of Internet presence that the coastal areas do because they generally don't sell to foreign clients. Often they don't even find their way onto the books of an estate agent, but simply change hands by word-of-mouth.

Northern Spain is often referred to as 'Green Spain', while central Spain is a high plateau, known as the *Meseta*, and has a continental climate. It can be extremely hot in the summer while winter can be very cold because of the height above sea level.

Property prices remain relatively low until you get within striking distance of Madrid and then they rise gradually the closer you get to the capital because those who live and work in Madrid (*Madrileños*) want somewhere relatively close for a weekend retreat.

If you are keen to build a new life in Spain and are prepared to learn Spanish, this could be an area worth looking at. Apart from Madrid, which is popular for short breaks, this isn't an area to invest in if you're looking for holiday rentals. Relatively few people who tour Spain visit these areas, most preferring to stay on the coast.

 ### 'Should I consider the north-west of Spain?'

This is another region of Spain which is rarely visited by foreign tourists but it is incredibly beautiful. The Atlantic coastline in particular, is stunning and comprises the autonomous regions of Galicia, Asturias, and Cantabria (total population 4.3 million). This area is beginning to increase in popularity and there are far more traditional properties for sale here, with availability increasing as you approach the coast. If you do an Internet search, which is possible for this area, you will find that prices are considerably lower in these areas. On the coast you will find a mix of traditional and new build properties, while inland there's a good choice of mainly old stone-built properties.

The north-facing coastline is dramatic and very beautiful but due to the influence of the Atlantic the climate is more like that of Brittany or Cornwall. It can feel almost like another country, especially in the Basque region, which borders Cantabria and where locals, particularly in inland areas, speak an entirely different language (Basque) and are fiercely independent. Castilian Spanish is, of course, also spoken here and if you plan to live in this region, you should be able to speak it fairly well as you're unlikely to find anyone who speaks English and won't find many other British expats living in this region.

Communications with the rest of Europe are good. There are airports and major ports at Bilbao and Santander with ferries to the UK. The main railway line from Madrid to Paris passes through the Pyrenees here. There are good motorway connections to south-west France and onwards to the French motorway network.

 ### 'What about the regions between the north-west and the north-east of Spain?'

As you move east, you are in the foothills of the Pyrenees, in the regions of the Basque Country (*País Vasco*), La Rioja, Navarre (*Navarra*) and Aragon with a total population of 4.2 million. You will find very few non-Spaniards living here. Communications with the rest of Spain are surprisingly good, particularly from the Basque Country, which has some of the best motorways in Spain and good air and sea links. La Rioja doesn't have an airport but does have good rail and road links, while the capital of Navarre, Pamplona, has an airport with daily flights to Madrid and Barcelona. There are two major routes across the Pyrenees; one on the Atlantic coast and one on the Mediterranean coast. The nearest airports are Bilbao to the west or Girona and Barcelona to the east.

If you choose to relocate to this area, you really would be stepping into the unknown and it's a good idea to rent a property in the area to familiarise yourself with the region and find the right property. The climate is varied, but in general, winters are cold and wet because of the mountains. The summers can be very hot but often coastal areas offer a welcome respite from the more extreme summer temperatures further south.

 ## 'What about the islands?'

There are two main groups of Spanish islands: the Balearics (population one million) and the Canaries (population two million). Many British citizens have either holiday or permanent homes on these islands.

Property prices in Majorca, the largest of the Balearic Islands, are relatively high, particularly in the northern part of the island which is an exclusive area, much favoured by the international jet-set. The southern part of the island has suffered the effects of tourism and over-development, but the island is trying to move away from the sun, sea and sangria image which it has enjoyed for so long. Palma, the capital, is home to one of the busiest airports in Spain and has good air connections with both Spain and the rest of Europe through a variety of scheduled, charter and low-cost and airlines.

Ibiza remains unique, it is one of the few places in the world where you will still find 'hippies' and it's renowned for its vibrant nightlife with Europe's best dance clubs. Property on Ibiza is the most expensive of all the Balearic Islands. Ibiza Town, in particular, is absolutely fascinating but the property prices reflect this. In the north of the island there are some very unimpressive resort areas such as San Antonio. Ibiza has its own international airport, which also serves the island of

Formentera and offers a range of scheduled, and charter flights. However, there are far fewer flights out of season and you must normally go via the mainland. There are frequent ferry services to mainland Spain and Majorca.

Menorca and Formentera are also very desirable islands, although they tend to be more popular for holiday homes rather than a permanent home. Ferry connections with the other islands are generally good but winter airline connections are far less frequent.

The other group of Spanish islands is of course the Canary Islands (population two million). These islands are fascinating with their volcanic black sand beaches and wonderful winter climate - they are closer to Africa than they are to Europe. However, they have been developed primarily for tourism which means that there is no shortage of modern resort-style properties, but very few old, traditional properties for sale.

Transport connections from the Canaries are generally good with a range of scheduled and charter airlines flying to the UK and other parts of Europe from the major airports, such as Gran Canaria, Lanzarote and Tenerife. The low-cost airlines are now beginning to offer flights to the Canary Islands from some UK airports. There are also inter-island ferry and jetfoil services although these vary depending on the time of year.

The real problem with island life is that communication with the rest of the world depends on airline or ferry services – you can't just jump in the car and drive to wherever you want to go. We have several friends who have lived on islands in various parts of the world and they all feel the same way – it can become an insular life that, from time to time, you just have to get away from.

Summary

Spain is a huge country which is heavily populated around the coastal areas but relatively under-populated in central and northern areas. The coastal areas are very cosmopolitan and it may be possible to buy property there without any need to learn Spanish. Move inland and you will be in a totally different environment living alongside local Spaniards whose families may have lived locally for generations. You will have to speak Spanish and work much harder to integrate into the local community.

There are certain questions which you need to ask yourself:

- **If I move to this area will I need to speak Spanish?**

- **Is this a tourist area?**

- **Are there any major plans for this area to change in the near future?**

- **What about transport links to and from this region, not only within Spain but also with the rest of Europe?**

- **What is the climate like in the region, and what will it be like in the winter?**

- **Will access to surrounding areas be easy during the winter months?**

- **Is there an expat community locally?**

- **Is the area cosmopolitan or more traditionally Spanish?**

- **If I need to work, is work available in this region?**

- **If I am buying property as an investment, will I get a return on that investment?**

- **Do I want to live the life of an expat in the sun, or could I cope with living in a more traditional Spanish area?**

Chapter 3

Which is the right property for me?

The first question you must ask yourself is what type of property you want to buy and where you would like it to be. Are you buying because you have enjoyed wonderful holidays in this area in the past? Do you really know the area or should you rent first to really determine that this the right location for you?

You really need to address the following questions:

- Is the new property going to be a holiday property?
- Do I want or need a return on my investment?
- Do I want to live in this property all the time?

'Do I want a property on the coast?'

This is the preferred choice for many northern Europeans who live in Spain permanently or for just part of the year. This is the Spanish dream for many of those who want a house or an apartment with a view of the sparkling Mediterranean Sea. It's a dream which many have realised. They have moved to a new country, they enjoy beautiful views and yet they can live in an area where they are surrounded by British expats and can speak English. Other northern Europeans such as the Germans, those from the Scandinavian countries and, increasingly, the Eastern European countries find they can do the same.

For some, however, living on the Costas could be a disastrous move because they might feel they were not living in a new country or experiencing a new culture. To do that you really need to move inland a little and avoid the coastal areas.

'Do I want to buy property on an urbanisation?

Many people who do buy on the coast buy a property which is part of an *urbanización* (urbanisation).

An urbanisation contains a selection of properties, which can be apartments, townhouses, villas or a mixture of all three. Property developers have bought the land and have (or should have) obtained detailed planning permission to build the properties.

This planning permission, known as a *plan parcial,* will usually refer to development which may occur over many years.

The buyers of these properties buy the individual property and the right to be a part of the community of owners and must follow the rules of the urbanisation.

Buyers of properties on urbanisations become part of a *comunidad de proprietarios* (community of owners) and are responsible for their individual property and the upkeep of the common parts of the urbanisation. This is a legal requirement so never buy in an urbanisation that doesn't have a community of owners. Every urbanisation is different, but all must have legal statutes and internal rules and your lawyer should check what your obligations as an owner will be. You can check the status of your intended purchase in the *registro de la propiedad* (Spanish property register). If it's not registered here, it's not legal. In many cases the roads which are built within the urbanisation – and which provide access to the various properties – also belong to the community of owners. If they need to be resurfaced or there are problems with things like drainage or lighting facilities, the local Town Hall will not pay for the repairs because they are effectively private. In the UK, they are called unadopted or private roads. Town Halls generally invest as little as possible in urbanisations, although they still collect taxes from the property owners!

The owners of these properties become shareholders in the urbanisation and have the right and a responsibility to attend an Annual General Meeting (AGM), the right to check any community records and the right to vote for a committee headed by an elected President (who has legal responsibility) to represent their interests. Among other things, this committee sets the urbanisation charges which are necessary to pay for the upkeep of the communal areas and essentially, the committee runs the development.

Unfortunately, many British people who buy in Spain do not realise their rights and responsibilities as property owners and do not even bother to attend the AGM. In our urbanisation of 60 apartments it is unusual to see more than 20 individual apartments represented at this important meeting. Non-attendance can mean that owners fail to elect a committee which represents their interests and so the job of looking after the community is sometimes handed over to a management company. In this case, the company sets the annual fees but, as they are in the business of making a profit, the fees will rise accordingly to cover their income. So it really is in your interests to attend this AGM.

Many of those who buy townhouses or independent villas on an urbanisation believe that they can make extensions and modifications in the normal way. Rules differ but, in general, you should seek permission from the committee of owners before you make any major changes to the property. This is so that they are in keeping with other properties on the urbanisation and, in theory, the committee could force an owner to return the property to its original state if they have made what are considered inappropriate modifications. This is a situation where planning permission does not just have to be obtained from the Town Hall but also from your neighbours – one good reason not to fall out with your neighbours.

Many urbanisations also contain individual villas with private gardens but even these come under the overall control of the committee, with things like the installation of a private swimming pool which requires both planning permission from the Town Hall and permission from the urbanisation committee.

Living in a community of owners means that there will be annual charges for the maintenance of the communal areas as mentioned above. This is often something which estate agents fail to mention and which can cause real problems. Ensure that your lawyer finds out exactly what your obligations are.

'Do I want a beachfront property?'

A beachfront property can seem like a dream come true and may look absolutely wonderful on your inspection trip in the spring, summer or autumn. However the Mediterranean is not always as placid as it looks in the tourist brochures. We have seen winter storms develop with enough force to destroy beachfront restaurants.

Before you consider a beachfront property you should check its distance from the beach and its age. The *Ley de Costas* (coastal law) has been in place since 1988 and prohibits building within 100 metres along the Spanish coast. So if your dream home is less than 20 years old and less than 100 metres from the beach, there's a strong possibility that it's illegal. An independent lawyer should carry out careful checks.

If the property has been approved by the coastal authorities, the most important question which you must ask about beachfront property is what is it built on? If the foundations are on rock you may have no problems in the future. If the property is built on sand, get a professional to check how secure the foundations are and what the damp-proof course is like (if there is one). We were shown beachfront properties with brass door handles which were already turning green after two years because of the moisture and salt inside the property.

When considering beachfront property make sure you consider what has already been built close by or what might be built in the future. In some parts of coastal Spain, land has been legally 'reclaimed' in order to build new marina style developments. However, in the process of reclamation the developers have actually changed the prevailing effects of the tidal currents which sometimes have a knock-on effect for other areas along the coast, such as flooding during winter storms. Even a surveyor could have difficulty in establishing whether this might be a problem. The best thing is to speak to long-term local residents who know the area well to discover whether local development is causing problems. For example, close to where we live, some new apartments have been built south-west of a dried up river bed. The locals said that nothing should ever have been built there because if the river floods, the ground floors of these apartments will also flood. In addition, the car park for this new development is underground, hollowed out from sand with concrete supporting walls. When it rains the water runs straight down the hillside and down the access ramp into the car park causing flooding. Many new properties have been built close to or even on top of what appears to be a dried up river bed. If there is severe snow in the hills behind the coast, and this happens every few years, that dried up river bed could become a raging torrent.

A new marina and an expensive residential development, Sotogrande, has been built 30 kilometres down the coast from where we live and this new development has already changed tidal flows. It has been built on a river estuary, and, in the process of creating a modern day Venice, the tidal flow of the sea can no longer move into the estuary so it's forced further along the coast. As a result, the old fishing village close to our apartment is now at severe risk of flooding during winter storms and has had to increase the height of its sea-wall.

'Do I want a property inland?'

Inland Spain is home to many major cities such as Madrid, Seville, Cordoba, Zaragoza and Tarragona, among others. Unless you are moving to a city for work purposes, they're not generally the first choice of the average expat. If you're buying a holiday property as an investment, cities are popular for short weekend breaks but do not tend to attract traditional holiday-makers who want two weeks self-catering accommodation so the market is quite a different one. Buy-to-let property for long-term rentals may be in demand for local businessmen and embassy staff, but it is unlikely that you would be able to use the property yourself.

Moving to the Spanish countryside is really for those expats who want to totally immerse themselves not just in a new country, but also in another culture and a new lifestyle. If you're able to adapt to this kind of challenge, your new life could be very rewarding. If you can't adapt, life can be very difficult indeed. It will be vital to learn Spanish because away from the tourist areas, few Spaniards speak English or any second language.

The other problem which can occur in really rural Spain is the limited access to local services. Some small villages may not even have services. Even with use of the Internet, which may be impossible to install, this can affect shopping, banking, healthcare and other vital services which many of us now take for granted. The nearest school might be a long distance from your home which would give a new perspective to the school run. You may not want to be 30 kilometres from the nearest town with good facilities, or 60 kilometres from the nearest hospital.

One of our friends, who is in her seventies, has adapted totally to living in a little *finca* in the middle of nowhere with limited access. She even sold the first *finca* which she bought to move even further inland. Her water supply comes from a well, electricity is supplied by solar power assisted by a petrol-driven generator and heating in the winter is a log-burner but she is a loner and loves the total isolation of the country. To be fair she is only 40 kilometres inland and she can drive back to the coast to buy petrol for the generator.

If the idea of living in the Spanish countryside appeals to you but you do not want to be totally isolated, this is possible in inland Spain even 30 kilometres from the coast where you will still be able to visit 'civilisation' when the need arises. However, many of your friends might be reluctant to visit you in the dark or in very bad weather. In daylight you can see the potholes in the road or in the dirt-track which would be invisible in the dark. Further inland you need to be very self-sufficient because you could be a long way from your nearest neighbour.

If you decide to buy inland in the Mediterranean areas, check how close the nearest trees are to your home. As summers become hotter with less rain, so the possibility of wildfires becomes stronger. These are happening with increasing regularity in Spain, Portugal and in Greece. This has happened close to where we live. One wonderful summer's day we suddenly heard a strange noise; it was a fire sweeping across the next hillside and, driven by a wind, it came charging down our valley which is a dried up river bed. As it got closer to the sea, the wind changed and it came sweeping back up the hillside, destroying everything in its path. Luckily the fire did not jump the road which separated us from the river bed otherwise the fire could have destroyed our gardens. By this time the *bomberos* (firemen) had arrived in helicopters which scooped up water from the sea to drop on the fires. At one point they asked if they could have access to the urbanisation so that they could put a pump attached to a hose into the swimming pool to obtain more water. The only serious damage was that three cars were destroyed and a lot of vegetation was totally burned but it was one of the most frightening moments of my life.

 ## 'Do I want an old property?'

If you wish to buy an old property which is full of character in order to fulfil your Spanish dream, your search may be more difficult if you want to be close to the sea. This is especially true in coastal areas where a property might be considered 'old' if it was built 40 years ago. There are generally a greater number of older properties in more rural inland areas.

In the coastal villages it's still possible to find old village houses or fishermen's cottages which are much older but they are often very small, because much of Spain was, until relatively recently, a very poor country. One of our friends has a wonderful village house but it has actually been created from three original houses. These houses often have an internal courtyard which, when renovated, could be decorated in a Moorish style. Many have a roof terrace which the original inhabitants would have used to dry the laundry, but it's very difficult to find a village-centre house which even has a small garden. When you do the price can be much higher. Only the rich had gardens.

There is also a potential problem with village or town centre properties, and that is the problem of noise. The local Spaniards are usually pretty sociable and do not tend to follow the same daily pattern that expats are used to. Spaniards are accustomed to a siesta after their main meal, which is around 2.30 p.m., and then after the work of the afternoon, they eat

71

dinner late and stay up until the early hours of the morning. Particularly in the south of the country, where the weather is generally warm for a large part of the year, they spend a lot of time outdoors, chatting to neighbours and meeting friends and family. Children are more accustomed to playing in the street, partly because of the lack of open spaces and private gardens in many of the old towns. All of this amounts to a lot of noise and if you come from a northern European country and are unused to such close contact with the local community it can come as something of a shock. We know people who have moved to village centre houses and have been unhappy because of the amount of noise they have encountered, simply because they're not used to it.

In the areas behind the coasts you will find old modernised or un-modernised *fincas*, but these are often very small. Depending on the region, you may also find old stone-built *cortijos* (country houses), the houses which were once occupied by wealthy landowners or vineyard owners.

In central Spain there are far more old properties to be found and if you avoid those areas which are within easy weekend travelling distance of Madrid, the prices can still be very reasonable.

In the north-west of Spain, or along the foothills of the Pyrenees, you will find old houses, both restored and un-restored and mostly stone-built, but prices depend on how accessible the house is or how close it is to a major tourist centre. Some of these properties can be very remote and this must be taken into account.

If you buy an old property which has been fully renovated, prices can be very expensive because they are few and far between. There are not many old renovated properties available, compared with the large numbers of new properties on the market. If you find a property that you would like to renovate, sign nothing until you have taken the advice of a surveyor or a builder who can give you an estimate of the real cost. If possible, get this estimate from a Spanish builder who knows the likely costs and understands the local way of building. It is however, true to say that the majority of immigrants to Spain prefer to buy a new property rather than go for an old one.

'How much renovation work do I want to do?'

Only you can decide this but even a relatively new property might require updating the kitchen or bathrooms, rewiring and redecoration. There is no shortage of tradesmen who will do the work and, if you prefer an English-speaking tradesman, they advertise in the local coastal English newspapers. I would advise you to find a bilingual project manager, which you can also find in the English newspapers, who will co-ordinate the work and will usually deal with local tradesmen who charge far less than their English counterparts.

You must build realistic renovation costs into your budget. If the agent shows you an older property and tells you the necessary work will cost a certain amount, then double this figure. Make sure you use tradesmen who will provide you with an *IVA* (VAT) invoice because this can be offset against any future Capital Gains Tax liability.

 ### 'Do I want a new property?'

If your dream is a new or almost new Spanish property then you really will be spoilt for choice in the coastal areas. Since the advent of mass tourism which began in the 1960s there has been an explosion of new development on the Costas. In fact the number of new home starts each year in Spain during the early part of the twenty-first century has been greater than the number in Germany, France and the UK added together. And this is in a country where the population is less than any of those three countries. The number has been as high as 800,000 new properties a year. Many of these are being built as second homes for Spaniards or for foreigners from northern Europe looking for a holiday home in the sun or an investment property. There are also more Eastern Europeans moving into Spain, which is rather ironic because many Brits are now buying holiday properties in Eastern Europe where the prices are similar to those in Spain a decade ago.

Nowadays, the majority of new homes are built on urbanisations comprising apartments, terraced townhouses, (known as *adosados*), or tiny detached villas on a very small plot of land which has just about enough room for the obligatory swimming pool. Two decades ago there were fewer urbanisations and far more detached villas built on large plots of land but prices have risen so much in that period that they are now surprisingly expensive. On the Costa del Sol for example, this type of property would be difficult to find for less than €700,000 (£500,000), this means that these properties have moved outside the realm of just being holiday homes and have turned into major capital investments.

Opposite our apartment there was a plot with existing planning permission for six villas which would have sold for approximately £400,000 each. When building started there was a change (initially without planning permission which is not really a problem in Spain), and as a result 16 terraced townhouses have been built which are selling for £250,000 each. Therefore, a fairly small plot which might have been worth £2.4 million to the developer when completed to the original plan is now worth potentially £4 million. It is not surprising that new detached villas on large plots are no longer being built apart from in very expensive areas where there is market for villas costing in excess of £1 million.

Many of the more recently built properties around the coasts can be very attractive and are cosmetically finished to a very high standard – even if the build quality may not be of the same standard. There are also many resale properties on the market so nobody will find it difficult to find the property of their dreams around the Mediterranean coast of Spain.

There are far fewer new build properties in inland Spain, even those areas relatively close to the coast, because the main market is for a property close to the sea. New build properties do exist close to the major cities where they are being built for the local population but often these new developments become very similar to suburban areas in the UK and tend not to be the stuff of dreams for most expats.

Many new properties are not built to a high standard. In the 1960s Spain discovered concrete and breeze blocks and these are now the main materials for construction. If these materials are used well, construction values can be very high but on occasions the walls between individual apartments or terraced houses can be only one breeze block thick and this may not be apparent on an initial viewing.

'What are the advantages of buying a new property off-plan?'

This is a route to the purchase of Spanish property which has been and still is followed by many new buyers particularly when time is on their side. Buying off-plan means that you often sign the initial sale documents before building has even started. You literally buy when you have just seen a plan of the development. The completion date can actually be several years ahead which can be good for long-term planning. During the building period you will be contracted to make staged payments – as agreed on the original documents – but you will not pay the total cost of your property until you actually move in.

The main advantage to you as the purchaser is that often the developer will set very competitive prices to encourage the sale of the first phase of a new development to get it off the ground. This means that you could be buying a real bargain and spreading your payments in stages. During the building period you are entitled to sell this unfinished property at the current market rate. In the past, during periods when property sales were booming, many people were able to realise a profit on a property which had not even been finished. The most important feature of buying in this way is that you must ensure that your staged payments are paid into a guaranteed bank account so that should the developer go bankrupt or fail to deliver in any other way you will get your money back.

Many speculators have made huge profits using this method of purchase. When you're told by the development company that the first phase is almost totally sold out and therefore you have to make a quick decision, it could mean that the first phase has been sold to speculators who will wish to re-sell before the properties are completed. Some speculators may buy up to 20 or 30 properties in a new development with a view to re-selling them at a profit during the construction period.

We once eavesdropped on a speculator who was making a call on his mobile at the next table to us at a beach restaurant. He was speaking to a colleague and reporting that he was about to put in an offer on 15 apartments further along the coast which were in the planning stage. There was no planning permission as yet, but if enough apartments were bought, planning permission should be a formality because people had already committed money to the project.

In an appreciating property market buying off-plan can be a real advantage because the completed property should be worth considerably more than the original price. However, if the market drops or collapses the end price could be lower. This happened in the early 1990s and it could happen again. If this happens, the speculators often have to get out quickly because they have overstretched themselves on borrowed money so prices can drop dramatically when the banks call in their loans.

Another benefit of buying off-plan can be the fact that you may be offered a choice of tiles for the kitchen or the bathrooms, or be able to specify other interior finishes you might want in your property. You might therefore have some input into the final appearance of your new home at no extra charge.

'What are the disadvantages of buying off-plan?

However good it might look on paper, there are a number of drawbacks to buying something that only exists as an artist's sketch and a blueprint. Firstly, you have no way of knowing what type of development you will finally move into. You have no way of knowing whether or not it will be inhabited by neighbours who live there virtually all the time or whether it may end up being primarily a holiday development.

You may be told that the property will be completed by a certain date in the future but almost without fail the builders will not meet this date. Everything in Spain is delivered late! This is the *mañana* culture and it can be very difficult to live with.

If you are buying in the first phase of a new development you have no way of knowing how long you might be living in the middle of a building site when you first move in. How long will it take before the communal grounds and swimming pools will be established? It could be two years or more.

You can't speak to existing residents (there are none) to ask how well the urbanisation is looked after, how well it is built or whether there are any other problems. We had one neighbour who bought off-plan in a new development close to us who realised that in an apartment block it might be possible to hear the toilet flush next door, but he had not expected to hear the original reason for the flush! He wanted to sell and he had only just moved in.

There is no indication at the planning stage what level of community charges will be levied, or whether they will be controlled by a good local committee or a management company.

Since the new properties have not been assessed for local taxes you have no way of knowing what the Town Hall might charge you for the equivalent of council tax.

You also have no way of knowing – and even your Spanish lawyer could have problems finding out – whether or not the off-plan property you want to buy has actually been sold. In a development close to us all the apartments and townhouses with the best views were marked on the plan as sold by the developers. As a result, new buyers were pushed towards their second choices and when these had been confirmed as sold, miraculously the sale of properties with the best views had fallen through and they were back on the market at a higher price.

'Is building a new property a possible option?'

This is not a common choice for many people who relocate to Spain. Plots of land which already have planning permission are available on some existing urbanisations and this could be the best choice for someone who really wants to build their own dream property. Often land is offered for sale with planning permission but your lawyer really does need to check this thoroughly. Land in Spain is classified as either urban, which means suitable for building or rural, which is virtually impossible to build on, although it may be possible to re-classify the land. However, it's very difficult to change the land's status from rural to urban. There are also *zones verdes* (green zones) which are areas assigned for gardens, parks and woods.

The process of building a new property is complex and you will need help from a good English-speaking Spanish lawyer. If you buy a building plot in an established urbanisation there should be approval in the *plan parcial* for a certain type of building. The *plan parcial* should be registered at the Town Hall and your lawyer should check that the use originally noted has not been changed and that your plot is not now in the middle of a *zona verde*, where building is prohibited.

You and your lawyer should also see the *Plan General de Ordinación Urbana (PGOU)*, the town plan. This is the town's 10-year plan and designates the various zones and defines their use. The plan must be approved by the regional government. The plan should be able to tell you what other properties could be built around your proposed building site. By studying this before you buy any land, you could discover that directly in front of the wonderful hillside site where you want to build your dream house there is outline planning permission for an apartment block which will not only block your view but could overlook your garden.

So many people have built beautiful properties in the coastal areas of Spain only to have their views, their lifestyle and their investment ruined by further development. A good example of this was on the other side of the valley from our home where a Scandinavian couple built a luxurious and very expensive villa which had amazing views of the coast and the mountains. Now it is surrounded by five-storey apartment blocks whose terraces look straight into their garden and most of their views have disappeared.

 ## Summary

Having decided where you might want to live in Spain, research which type of area and property is right for you. With so much to choose from, it can be hard to know what to choose – which is why I always advise you to rent before you buy.

These questions will stop you from throwing your money away and help you determine what might suit your future needs:

- **Where do I want to buy within my chosen region? On the coast or inland?**

- **Do I want to be in a busy area or somewhere more rural?**

- **Do I want to live in an expat community or would I prefer to be in a Spanish area?**

- **Do I want to renovate an old property?**

- **Do I want to buy off-plan and can I wait until the property is completed?**

- **Do I want to build my own property?**

Glossary

urbanización	urbanisation or development of apartments, townhouses, villas or a combination of all three.
registro de propiedad	Spanish property register
Ley de Costas	coastal law
plan parcial	the municipal plan which shows how land is classified and what type of long-term planning permission has been granted
Plan General de Ordenación Urbana/PGOU	town's 10-year development plan
zonas verdes	green zones
adosados	townhouses
fincas	farmhouses
cortijos	country houses
bomberos	firemen

Chapter 4

How do I find my ideal property?

Q *'Where should I begin my search?'*

Unless you are totally familiar with a region you think you might like, the first step must be to buy some guide books or use the Internet to get a feel for the area. The Internet also has details of local estate agents and accessing their sites can give you an idea of how much your ideal property might cost and you can compare the prices of similar properties on offer from other agents. This can help to give you an overall picture of the area and the property available. Websites can also provide information about local services, distances to major towns and transport links such as airports and good roads or railway services.

'Should I go to Spanish property exhibitions in the UK?'

Property exhibitions are useful because they will give you a feel for the country and its various regions and what is available to buy. However, you need to remember that most of the exhibitors are there to try to sell you a property. Take their information on board as part of your research but try not to sign anything until you have had time to assess the information away from the exhibition environment.

 ## 'Should I take the offer of a free or subsidised inspection trip to view property?'

These trips will only be available if you are buying in a coastal area. There are no inspection trips to inland Spain because as yet, no property developers are intensively working in the inland areas.

These trips are organised and often funded either by developers – who are obviously keen to sell their properties – or by estate agents, who may be acting for these developers and who may be being paid a higher than normal rate of commission for any properties sold. Remember that if you go on one of these trips, you're not free to look at any properties you want to, simply at the properties that the developers or agents want to sell.

We had friends who went on an inspection trip. They were met at the airport by the agent and driven to their hotel. There was no way that they could rent a car and be independent because the agents did not want them contacting another agent or looking for property independently. He wanted his commission and to do that he had to sell specific properties.

For two days they were met at breakfast by the agent and taken to see potential properties. At all times his clipboard was in his hand with the appropriate documents in case they wanted to sign an agreement to buy. They had lunch with the agent and then dinner and at the end of the day they were virtually escorted back to their bedroom and locked in to make sure that they could not escape and speak to anyone else. Despite the fact that we, as friends, lived locally they could not contact us without some difficulty and they certainly could not visit us because we might introduce them to another agent. Although taking up the offer of an inspection trip does not commit you to buy a property, the organisers are very keen to sell their properties and may not give you very much time (if any) to look around the area at your leisure.

Our friends bought a holiday apartment, off-plan, during their trip and to be fair they appear to be very happy! They did however buy in a very good development built by a well-respected English property developer.

Personally I would never get involved in a free or subsidised inspection trip. I worked in marketing and PR for many years and respect the familiar concept that there is no such thing as a free lunch! Anyone who does buy on one of these trips is probably paying over the odds because they are subsidising all those who have not bought. If you do not buy you are helping to push up the prices of all the other properties, new or resale, because the developers and agents have to increase the asking prices to pay for these subsidised trips.

 'When is the best time of year to look for property?'

There is no definitive answer to this question. At the height of the season you will see properties at their best, the weather should be wonderful, all the restaurants and bars will be open and the swimming pools will be blue and inviting. The downside is that many resale homes may be occupied with holiday rentals and the agent may not be able to show it to a potential purchaser. Obviously new, unoccupied property can be viewed but you may not be able to see everything on offer and so compare new and resale properties.

One of the best times to view is spring or autumn. Resale rental properties are likely to be empty and therefore available to view. The weather is usually good, you don't have to view properties in the extreme heat of the summer and at these times of the year you should have easy access to all the property which is on the market.

If you're planning to relocate permanently to Spain, you really need to view your potential purchase during the winter months, between the middle of November and the end of March. If you love it then you will love it all year round. The weather in Spain is not always the weather you see on TV relocation programmes or in the photographs in relocation magazines. The sky is not always blue, on the coast it rains and inland the rain often turns to snow. Remember also that during the winter months many restaurants and bars close, swimming pools in urbanisations are sometimes left untended and turn into green pools of slime and many properties are simply left shuttered and empty.

In simple terms if you want an investment property which you will let, then view it at the height of the season so that you can see the potential for your tenants. If you want to relocate permanently, see the property in the winter so that you can evaluate whether you could live there. If in doubt, rent a property first before you commit your hard-earned cash to the wrong home.

'How do I find a good estate agent?'

Many people buy a holiday home in an area they're already familiar with, often while on holiday themselves. Although there's no harm in house-hunting this way, if you're considering a permanent move then once you've done your research the next step really should be to rent in your chosen area and find a good local estate agent, known as an *inmobiliaria*.

If you aren't able to rent first and you have to depend on finding an estate agent on the Internet, you need to be far more careful. The larger agents now have a massive online presence as well as advertising in the property magazines and on UK television. Remember that this level of advertising is expensive so the agent will be making a good profit – thanks to people like you, the potential buyer. Remember too that you can't tell over the Internet whether a company, large or small, is a reputable and experienced one. Always check any information they give you and never part with any money without consulting an independent lawyer first.

When we first looked at property in Spain I had done all my homework on the Internet and we went to our chosen area to look at property. The agents who had been briefed by e-mail from the UK duly turned up to take us to view property. I thought I had given a fairly tight brief – we wanted a character property, hopefully with a bit of land, probably a few years old in an established area close to the sea.

The first agent knew the area quite well and showed us some established properties which were either very uninspiring and inexpensive or wonderful and right at the top end of our budget, or even beyond our budget when she always said 'Try an offer'. The other properties she took us to were all new and to be bought off-plan. Another day and another agent turned up in a very flashy car. He had received the same brief and represented one of the biggest agents in our part of Spain. However, he had driven 30 kilometres down the coast for our meeting and didn't know the local area well and had to use a map to find his way around. He only took us to one resale property but knew exactly where all the new properties were. It was actually through him that we found a new development which looked wonderful and we made our first ever offer on Spanish property. It was all so easy because we could use our English credit card to pay the holding deposit. Does this not remind you of time-share selling?

This was the purchase we were lucky enough to get out of, thanks to a good independent lawyer. We did not lose any money from our deposit but we did have to pay the lawyer's fees. If we had we used the lawyer who was working for the developer we might not have been able to extricate ourselves from the purchase so easily.

Why do I make these points about estate agents? Simply because estate agents in Spain are very different from those you might have encountered in the UK. To begin with most UK agents often work hard on a relatively low commission rate. When we sold in London we negotiated a rate of 2 per cent on a sole agency basis. In Spain the commission rate on a resale property is usually 5 per cent. Although in theory this is paid by the seller, it's often incorporated into the price, meaning that the buyer effectively pays. The sellers will often be asked what price they want to achieve and the agent will then add the commission to this price to set the asking price for the property. On new property the commission can be much higher - 10 per cent or more, so there is a real incentive to the agent to clinch a sale of a new property. When the market is buoyant the agents can and do make a lot of money.

When we were considering a move further inland we found a very good agent who showed us many houses which we loved, but she admitted over lunch that the agency which she worked for only sold resale property because they were not prepared to get into the cut-throat business of the new property market.

In the new-build market, developers have to sell to recoup their investment and building costs. So they try to persuade local estate agents to enter into an agreement whereby if the agent sells a certain number of properties in a particular development during an agreed period, the rate of commission will be much higher than 5 per cent. This is why many agents aggressively push sales of these new properties. However, at the end of the day it is the purchaser who ends up paying the increased commission and the price of the new properties rises accordingly. Those re-selling property also think their homes should increase in value at the same rate, so overall the price of houses increases until the buyers stop buying.

When we were selling one of our apartments there was a local English estate agent who came round to view the property. He gave us a valuation and said that we should not worry because he had many clients who were just crying out for a property like ours. For the next few months we saw him bringing potential clients to the new properties which were being built on the hillside behind us but he never brought a single potential client to our home! I can only assume that it was good for him to have our property on his books or as a photograph in his window, but he was more interested in selling new property at a higher rate of commission.

Another local agent stood in our kitchen during a viewing and told his clients that they ought to be looking at the new apartments on the other side of the road. I was in the room at the time and I almost threw him and the potential purchasers out of my home. Now that there is a slightly more difficult property market in south-west Spain, that particular agency has gone bankrupt and out of business.

You must also remember that in any property transaction the estate agent is working for the vendor, whether that is an individual or a property developer. However you, as a buyer, are also a client. If the agent does not achieve a sale they make no money so, on occasions, an imaginative use of the truth on the part of the agent could achieve a sale.

Take everything they say with a very large pinch of salt. Statements such as: 'the field next door could never be built on' or 'the hillside in front is too steep to allow building' or indeed any other statement which the agent might make about a property should always be checked out by an independent lawyer. If the field or the vineyard next door looks untended, it may be that the owner is going to try to have it re-classified as urban land and sell it for development. It would be worth more money to the owner if it's classified as urban.

You owe it to yourself to shop around with different estate agents, all of whom should have a detailed and concise brief about what you really want and should stay within your declared budget. You should never tell an agent the top end of your budget because many will only show you properties of that price or higher and will often say that the vendor 'might accept an offer'. If you're well prepared and the agent realises you know what you are talking about, you're more likely to be shown the right property. If you come across as naïve and unsure about what you want that is the time that agents will show you the properties which they most want or need to sell. Good preparation will also help you to ask the right questions and spot the incorrect or uncertain answers.

As I said earlier, the first step is to find a good estate agent preferably one who has professional qualifications. Agents are not regulated by the government in Spain but if you can find one with the qualification *Agente de la Propiedad Inmobiliaria* (*API*) or *gestor Intermediario de la Promociones y Edificaciones* (*GIPE*), at least you can rest assured that they have their own regulatory body. If the agent has either of these on his letterhead or on the property descriptions, you should have no problems. Beware the large numbers of unqualified, inexperienced or even amateur estate agents scattered around the country, many of whom are trying to make a living out of buying and selling property. The industry is not regulated as it is in the UK.

You should also check that the agent has a bonded bank account in which any money you pay as a deposit will be held. This essentially means that when you pay the deposit it will be held in this account in your name and in the agent's name but only released on your authorisation when the sale is completed. There have been occasions when potential buyers have paid their deposit only to find later that when the sale falls through they can't get their deposit back. Of course they could take the agent to court but legal proceedings in Spain often take many years.

'What other services should a good estate agent offer?'

Having found a good agent (or agents) you can then enjoy the exciting process of looking for your ideal home. A good estate agent should be working for both the vendor and the buyer and will be worth their weight in gold. Unless you buy the agent will make no commission, but with the much higher levels of commission in Spain your chosen agent should be prepared to offer some type of after-sales service. After all, if you find a property priced at €200,000 and you make a quick decision the agent will earn €10,000. Surely for this kind of fee they should offer some kind of after-sales service?

Representatives of some large estate agencies may not offer the following services because their prime objective is to sell the property and earn their commission from the vendor. When you sign on the dotted line their involvement might come to an end so make sure you know what they do offer, if anything, and get it in writing. Many sales representatives of both large and small agencies do not even understand the finer details of selling property in Spain. They are simply programmed to get your signature on the sales documents so that they can earn their bonus from the sale - the commission goes to the company which is employing them.

A good agent acting for the seller and the buyer should:

- be able to introduce you to a trustworthy, independent, bilingual lawyer who will act solely for you.
- guide you through the legal process and help you to obtain the necessary legal documents.
- be bilingual and able and happy to help you register all the proper documents at the local Town Hall.
- help you to transfer the utility bills, telephone service etc. into your name.
- be able to take you to a local bank where you can open an account having been introduced by the agent.
- know the local area very well so that they can quickly find the type of property you want to buy.

A good agent could in the end become a friend and you will in turn recommend their services to other potential clients.

Q 'What should I take with me when I'm property searching?'

If you are outside your home country you will have your passport which proves who you are should you make an offer on a property. Any other documentation can be presented when necessary. There is no need to carry a full file of documents.

Q 'When should I open a Spanish bank account?'

There is no need to open a bank account in Spain until you know where you are going to live. If you find the right property a deposit can be arranged within a few days through an international bank transfer from your local account or even instantly on a credit card through some agents. Even the complete buying process can be completed without having a Spanish bank account. We know many owners of Spanish property who do not even have a bank account in Spain. They can withdraw cash from the ATM machine using a British card and their utility bills are sent to their UK address. However, some utility companies require Spanish bank account details so that bills can be paid directly. You can set up direct debits for the utilities and make sure that bills are paid automatically. This way you avoid having your services disconnected if, for example, a bill goes astray. This happens far more easily in Spain than the UK and no-one wants to arrive at their holiday home to discover there is no electricity, water or telephone, particularly if they are letting the property.

There is no need to register as a foreigner in Spain until you have an address there, but before you can purchase a property you must have a *Número de Identificación de Extranjero*, which is known as an *NIE*. This is a foreigner's identification number and identifies you to the tax authorities. The number must go on the *escritura* and is needed for all kinds of official business in Spain, so it is worth applying for one as soon as possible.

 Summary

No matter what type of property you want to buy make sure you find an estate agent who specialises in that market. Make sure they're working for you as the client, especially if they're taking a hefty cut of the sale. Prepare a concise brief for the agent and ensure that your chosen agent finds the dream property for you.

Make sure you ask yourself:

- **What is it exactly that I'm looking for?**
- **Should I visit a property exhibition in the UK?**
- **Do I want to look for property whilst on holiday or would it be better to rent in the area first?**
- **Where do I want my property to be located?**
- **Do I have all the necessary documentation?**
- **Do I know what the area is like out of season?**

Make sure you ask your agent:

- **Do you have properties on your books that fit my strict criteria?**
- **Are you bilingual?**
- **How well do you know my specific search area?**
- **What after-sales services can you provide?**
- **Can you introduce me to an independent, bilingual lawyer?**

Glossary

inmobiliaria	estate agent
Agente de la Propiedad Inmobiliaria (API)	recognised estate agent qualifications (not obligatory)
gestor Intermediario de la Promociones y Edificaciones (GIPE)	recognised estate agent qualifications (not obligatory)
Número de Identificación de Extranjero/NIE	Foreigner's Identification Number

Chapter 5
How do I know if I've found what I want?

Only you know the answer to this question but, in my experience, people generally know from instinct that they have found their dream home. However, there are still questions to be asked and these depend on your reasons for buying.

The crucial questions now are:

- If you plan to live there all year round, will this property meet all your needs?
- If you are buying as a buy-to-let investment, will your potential tenants think the way you do about the property?

This chapter will help you address the critical questions you must ask yourself at this stage.

Q '*I have found an ideal property, should I make a quick decision?*'

The answer to this is almost always a firm 'no'. Unless the property ticks all the boxes two, or even three times over, there will be another one as good, if not better, just around the corner. The only time I would advise against this is if, through a combination of good local knowledge (which can only be gained by renting locally for a period) and thorough research you know that the asking price is really competitive and the property is a real bargain. If this is the case make a quick offer. Resist the temptation to make a quick irrational offer.

The agent will want you to make a decision because they want to clinch a sale but remember that you're in a strong position. Property in Spain and in many other parts of Europe, is not selling as quickly as it has done in previous years, despite what the media might try to make us believe. I know people who have had their property on the market for two years or more without a single offer because the asking price is too high and they are waiting for the market to improve so that they can get the price they want. The continued building of new developments and an increase in available resale properties means that it's a buyer's market in Spain, where too many properties are competing for too few buyers. Generally it's better to take as much time as you need to fully consider your decision before making a commitment. Never allow the agent to persuade you to make a quick decision. You need to be sure that your offer is on the right property.

Q '*Does this property work for its intended purpose?*'

If you plan to live in Spain 52 weeks a year and you want to live in a coastal area, then a villa or a townhouse with a private patio or garden in an urbanisation is a great choice for most people. Such properties will give you lots of personal space and privacy. Better still, is a detached villa on its own land, if you can afford the high prices which these now command. Apartments can be more of a problem particularly if you're surrounded by other apartments which are rented to holidaymakers during the high season. If you're living and working in Spain or even if you're retired, the sound of holidaymakers partying till the early hours of the morning can become irritating. This potential problem may not be apparent if you're looking at property out of season – when there are few or no tourists about.

The style of the property is also an important consideration for permanent living. The acres of white marble used in many coastal properties for flooring, looks beautiful and has a wonderful cooling effect in the heat of the summer. However, in winter it can produce a refrigerating effect. It's far better if you can find a property with terracotta tiled floors or wood floors as these surfaces are warmer in winter.

Marble floors in apartments can also cause problems as they don't provide sufficient insulation against noise and you will not realise this on a viewing visit. It will only become apparent when you move in and someone is walking around in hard-soled shoes in the apartment above in the early hours of the morning, or when a new set of holidaymakers arrive late at night and decide to re-arrange the furniture by dragging it across the floor!

On the coast it will be more difficult to find a property without marble floors, but if you move inland you will find older, traditional properties, either in the villages or in the country, which have a more traditional structure with tiled floors and, depending on the area, thick stone walls.

If you want to buy a property which will be primarily a holiday home, the features of your chosen property might be very different from those you might choose if you plan to live in the property permanently. A holiday property might only be used during the Spring to Autumn period therefore marble floors, which would be cold in the winter, will not be a problem - in fact they could be an advantage, helping to keep your property cool, and they look so impressive. South-facing rooms would also be a positive feature because for a short holiday period it's wonderful to have as much direct sunlight as possible.

In fact if you plan to let the property in the summer and live there yourself in the winter south-facing rooms or terraces are a really good thing to have. Your summer visitors will bake in the sun during their two-week holiday, which is after all what they paid for, and you will benefit from the winter sun when you occupy the property. Whatever you do, don't make the mistake which several of our friends have made. Do not glass in a south-facing terrace or balcony unless all the windows open fully or better still can be removed in the summer. All you will do is to create a greenhouse which is unusable in the heat of the summer.

If you're looking for a holiday home or rental investment the location is vital. Holidaymakers like to be close to the beach, the shops, bars and restaurants and they like sun-baked terraces, gardens and swimming pools. The majority of tourists who visit Spain stay in the coastal areas so an apartment or town house in a good urbanisation with a wonderful communal swimming pool would be ideal. If you're hoping for a rental return on the property then a large two-bedroom apartment or townhouse with a living room large enough to have a sofa bed will achieve the same rental as a three-bedroom property. The former will sleep six, the latter will sleep eight but most groups of eight or more would probably prefer to rent a villa because it will have more space both inside and out.

If you decide that your own needs would be better served by buying a villa but you might still want to let it during the peak holiday season, then any villa you consider must have its own private swimming pool. Holidaymakers expect a pool, although when calculating your rental return you should factor in the cost of swimming pool maintenance if you're not there to do it yourself.

 ## 'Is the location right?'

If it is purely for holidays for yourself, your family and may be used for holiday rentals, then you need to have south-facing rooms to catch all the sunlight. If your chosen property is a townhouse then a south-facing terrace or garden is a definite advantage. If the property is a villa, a private swimming pool is essential.

If you plan to live in your property permanently, your requirements will be very different. Make sure you have rooms which face east or west or, better still, have a covered or vine-shaded terrace so that you can avoid the blistering heat of the summer sun. If you're buying an apartment or a townhouse in an urbanisation avoid any properties which face directly onto the communal swimming pool. The noise in the busy holiday season can be unbearable and it will continue until the early hours of the morning even if the community rules say that the pool should not be used after 10 p.m. in the evening. The majority of holidaymakers do not read the rules.

Whatever type of property you buy, if it is for year-round occupation a log-burning stove is a real plus, if not essential.

Wood is by far the cheapest way to provide warmth on winter evenings which, even in most parts of coastal Spain, can be cold. Further inland and in central Spain, winters are usually very cold indeed. In most of the country there is no mains gas so gas-fired central heating and hot water is provided using bottles of propane or butane gas.

We have one friend who inherited this method of heating in her new home and she was using virtually one bottle of gas per day during the winter at the cost of €25.00 per day. However, gas heating is far less expensive than electricity which can be prohibitively expensive during the winter. So a log-burner makes sense.

It's important to remember not to leave logs around the log-burner throughout the year. It may look very decorative but sometimes the logs host termites which exist in many parts of southern Europe. The termites can move from the logs intended for burning and penetrate the softwood door frames on your home. These can be turned to powder very quickly and we know of people who have had to renew the door frames because of termite attack. It is not all bad news however because as yet, there is not a species of termite which attacks UPVC windows or concrete!

'How far is it from the nearest town?'

If you plan to live permanently in your new home this may or may not be important, depending on your circumstances. If you have your own transport you can plan to make one or two visits a month to the nearest large supermarket. Local shops can sometimes be expensive especially if they are in popular tourist areas. Remember that you may also need to be able to get to schools and medical facilities as well as leisure facilities such as golf courses, bars and restaurants. A holiday investment property may not need to be too close to the nearest town as long as there are reasonably good local facilities. Some holidaymakers actually enjoy being a bit remote for a couple of weeks - it is part of the holiday - but many appreciate a small local supermarket and easy access to bars and restaurants.

'How far is it from the nearest school?'

This is a very important question for young families with children. In the coastal areas there is a strong possibility that there will be a school bus which will take your children to school so all you need to do is to take your children to the nearest pick-up point and collect them at the end of the day. However, in more remote country areas you may find that a lot of time is taken up by the school run if there is no school bus, so it's something worth considering before you make your final decision on the property purchase.

'How far is it from the nearest hospital?'

Not all major towns have their own hospital or one which can provide the appropriate treatment which you might need. This is particularly important if you have young children, you're elderly or require ongoing or specialist treatment. Where we live on the Costa del Sol, the nearest major hospital is 45 minutes away but it does not have all services. One of our friends needed hospital treatment and the nearest hospital which could provide it was in Malaga which meant that his wife had to drive for almost an hour and a half to visit. The husband of another friend had cancer and the nearest hospital which could provide treatment was in Seville. On occasions visits required an overnight stay in a hotel.

'How far is it to transport connections?'

In coastal areas you will probably not be far from a reasonably efficient, if slow, bus service, but inland this might not be so easy. The rail service is generally good between major towns and cities. Access to airports which have good connections to other parts of Europe is also an important consideration, particularly if you're planning to work in Spain and need to travel to other areas of Spain which aren't popular holiday areas. Depending on your destination, you may need to fly via Madrid or Barcelona. For example, I was once asked to visit Vienna for a business meeting and the only way I could fly to Vienna from Malaga was via Madrid, Barcelona or London on scheduled flights at a very high cost. However, it's always worth checking as Malaga airport in particular is increasing the number of direct flights to some European destinations.

'What are the neighbours like?'

You can only find this out by going back to your chosen property without the estate agent and speaking to some of the people who already live there. If you buy off-plan you have no way of knowing who your neighbours might be and if you buy in a remote country area your nearest neighbour might be some distance away so this question might be irrelevant.

'What is the area like during the winter?'

If you speak to your future neighbours they should be able to answer this question but only if they live in their property all year. The only way to really find out is to rent first and get to know the area in all seasons. There are many urbanisations in the coastal areas which are run by the community of owners primarily as summer destinations and this could seriously affect you if you decide to live there all year round. Many owners regard their properties as investments for a rental return and they and their families only use the property in the early or late summer - to them winter is irrelevant.

Often at the end of the summer season the community might decide by a democratic vote to switch off the pumps and filtration systems for the communal swimming pools. To keep them running all year is a cost to the community and all owners are jointly responsible for these costs. The decision will have been made by a majority of owners, but many of them will be absent during the winter and will not see the swimming pools turn into slimy green lagoons which are extremely unattractive and remain like that for several months. In the spring the pool will be emptied, cleaned and returned to its former pristine condition in readiness for the summer season which generally starts at Easter and lasts until the end of October.

You need to know that this might happen if you plan to live permanently in your new property. You might not want to look out on a green slime pool in the winter! You can only find this out by talking to existing owners and getting an honest opinion or alternatively, you should view prospective properties during the winter months.

It's also a good idea to check with existing residents about the number of people who live in the urbanisation all year round. You might be quite happy to see all the properties around you closed up and shuttered for four to five months of the year, but equally you might find it very depressing to live in what is effectively a ghost town. You might also find that many of the restaurants and bars, even those in the nearest town, close during the winter so even if you want to escape and socialise there could be nowhere to go to.

You should also find out if the communal gardens are maintained throughout the year or only for the summer season because untended gardens can be very unattractive.

The above comments refer to properties in coastal areas. Should you choose to live in inland Spain your life could be very different.

In some areas life is even more lively out of the traditional holiday season because many of the local population move to the coastal areas in the summer to find work. They return home at the end of the autumn and stay until early spring when the seasonal work starts again. As a result, many inland areas have more going on during the winter months.

Many small towns in the regions just inland from the Mediterranean coast have the most amazing Christmas decorations organised by the local authority and sometimes the local population. For many locals the winter is the time when the town comes alive again because the whole family is together. This is just one occasion when speaking Spanish means having more fun! If your Spanish is good enough and you have been accepted by the local population, you can join in with celebrations and learn about the different way that Spaniards, for example, celebrate Christmas. These are all things which make life in a new country a lot of fun and very rewarding.

If you find the right kind estate agent in any area of Spain who specialises in inland property, they will happily explain what life is like in these small inland towns and villages out of season. The personal experiences of many of these agents could be enough to convince you that this is where you want to live. A good agent like this is a real find but isn't typical of the Brits who are trying to sell property on the Spanish Costas. Most potential buyers don't meet the agents who love Spain and want to encourage other Brits to appreciate the country at its best. They can sometimes be found by doing an Internet search for country property in your chosen region.

In central or northern Spain, it's more difficult to find an estate agent who speaks English. If you're really interested in these areas, it is worth learning some Spanish before you go looking for a property. That way you can find out the information you need, although it is important to realise that you will be much more of a pioneer in this kind of area where properties change hands through word-of-mouth and may not be advertised in the traditional way. You might even find it difficult to find an estate agent in the true sense of the term.

'If it's a new property can the local infrastructure cope with the development?'

This is a very difficult question to answer and one your lawyer should check with the local and regional authorities. In theory, if there is a *plan parcial* and the urbanisation is legal, then the infrastructure should be sufficient. However, there are many instances when this does not work as it should. For example, our apartments are in an urbanisation which has a *plan parcial*, but that was created 20 years ago. At the time, we had drainage facilities, electric cabling, water supply and all the other modern facilities which would be expected according to that plan. However over the years the plan has changed.

Where there was once 'green space', developers are now building 250 apartments. Where there was planning permission for six villas the developers are now building 16 townhouses. We have already had problems with our water supply and this could get worse in the future because the original plan did not take account of the density of building which is now taking place.

Spain in the summer can be very arid and water is often at a premium in some areas.

In the Spanish press there have already been articles which have highlighted the fact that within 10 to 15 years there may not be enough fresh water to cope with the amount of development in Valencia. As a result the authorities are looking into the possibility of installing desalination plants.

The other potential problem with the water supply is that it might depend on electric pumps bringing the water from an underground reservoir. During a power cut you will have no water and power cuts in Spain are fairly frequent. This happened in an urbanisation close to us where most of the water came from an underground well. It could cope with the initial development but, because this area has spectacular views over the coast and views mean profit, new development has now resulted in so many new properties being built that water now has to be pumped in from the surrounding areas. No problem until there is a power cut.

The ultimate nightmare is when all the new properties are occupied at the same time and every property is making a demand on the infrastructure. This may never happen as many are only occupied for short periods as holiday properties, but it's worth bearing in mind.

'What plans exist for future development in the area and how well will it be controlled?'

This very important question must be asked by an independent Spanish lawyer. He should check the *plan parcial* to see what future development is planned. You should ask for a copy of this plan and keep it on file.

Even this might not be a total safeguard because planning permission in some parts of Spain can suddenly appear where none was before, or the status of land can suddenly change so that planning permission can be granted. Unlike the UK, the new plans are rarely posted on a local notice board to allow existing residents to object. This is why it is important to have a copy of the *plan parcial*. If you discover that your property is going to be surrounded by a new development which will completely obstruct the views you thought you were buying, you will need to produce the documents to prove that the new development was never planned. Otherwise you will not have a legal leg to stand on.

We almost fell foul of this. The first property that we made an offer on was on a hillside with the most amazing views of the sea. Directly in front was a very steep hillside and the estate agent assured us that nothing could possibly be built in front because the hillside was too steep. However there is a substance called dynamite and Spanish developers have learned how to use it to best effect. It's now possible to create flat platforms on an otherwise inaccessible hillside so that other properties can be built which could obstruct the view from your home.

During the worst period of potentially illegal development close to us when life was becoming very difficult, the President of our urbanisation was continually delivering *denuncias* (reports of crimes or illegal activities) to the Town Hall but as soon as she left they were more than likely consigned to the waste bin. To be fair the local mayor did follow up on some of these *denuncias* and visited the site but everything the residents had complained about had been miraculously cleaned up or repaired. The broken pavements, broken manhole covers, mud on the roads, and many other things were all sorted out just one day before the visit of the mayor.

Another friend bought a villa which had the most amazing views I have ever seen in my life. The vista ranged from Estepona across to the Riff Mountains and the north coast of Africa and Gibraltar to the west. The hillside in front of the villa was precipitous and everyone said 'You're so lucky, nothing could ever be built in front of you' but sadly, it has, thanks to dynamite. There are now luxury apartments directly in front of this property which partially spoil the view from this amazing villa. Happily he sold the property before the new building started.

Other friends bought and restored a wonderful old *cortijo*, a country house which was more than 300 years old. It was virtually in the middle of nowhere and had spectacular views over the surrounding countryside and the sea. The access road was little more than a dirt-track and was a nightmare in bad weather. This property has now been surrounded by a new urbanisation of expensive villas and townhouses which has taken away their solitude, many of their views and, to add insult to injury, the urbanisation has actually been named after their property. The only benefit to their property is that there is now a made up road which leads to their gate and they have mains drainage. However, their local taxes will undoubtedly be higher because the land has been urbanised.

In the process these new developments can wipe thousands of euros off the value of the existing properties while often adding many more thousands to the pockets of the developers. If your chosen property has wonderful views but there is undeveloped land close by, you should proceed with caution as eventually, the land is likely to arouse the interest of a developer. Even if there is an apparently inaccessible hillside behind or in front of you, do remember that with the help of dynamite that hillside could also be a building site - especially if it has wonderful views.

 ### 'How can I check the build quality?'

If your chosen property is a resale you should pay a surveyor to check for possible structural problems. If he is a local Spanish surveyor, he will know the area and may be aware of any possible problems. You can also ask other residents about their experiences and whether they have noticed possible problems. You need to find out whether or not there is good noise insulation laterally or, if your choice is an apartment, laterally and vertically. Are there any problems with plumbing, water supplies, care of the communal facilities or indeed any other factors which might affect your investment?

It's absolutely vital that you return to the property as many times as you need to and check the details you did not notice first time around. Any good estate agent will not hurry you around. We did that with one property which we absolutely fell in love with. It was on high ground with amazing views but when we looked in more detail, we noticed that there was a 2 centimetre gap under the front door. In the garden there was a ring of stones round every tree and bush towards the hillside. The wonderful balustrade on the edge of the terrace, which was the barrier between the house and the view, had serious gaps underneath. The house and the terrace were potentially slipping over the edge of the ridge.

Outside the front door there was a water channel which ran under the paved area to allow rainwater to run down the road but the actual entrance to the house was 10 feet below the road level and if the channel became blocked, the area outside the front door would probably flood.

The view was amazing then, but the hillside in front now contains hundreds of apartments. How much damage has been done to the already fragile state of the terraces and garden by blasting that hillside? We already lived in the area so we were able to talk to locals and discovered that this particular urbanisation was the one which had insufficient water to meet its needs and water had to be piped in from other areas. Had we been your average property viewer we might have seen this villa and made a quick offer which we would eventually have regretted. We gave ourselves time to revisit the house and ask questions and, as a result, totally rejected this house, despite the wonderful views.

This is another reason why I would always advise everyone to rent first. With the benefit of time on your side, you can return to view a property several times before committing yourself to a purchase. If you are paying thousands of euros on a property, why make a decision based on a half hour visit?

'How can I check the build quality of a new property?'

If the property is new or you are buying off-plan this is much more difficult. A brand new property could seem beautifully finished with state-of-the-art kitchens and bathrooms, wall-to-wall marble floors and a wonderful luxury ambience but what lies underneath the surface? An off-plan property purchase is even more difficult to evaluate because it does not exist at the time of purchase. The majority of buyers buy what they actually see and not what lies below the surface of the property which has been built because that is invisible to the buyer.

You may wonder why I say this. It's because we have seen at first hand how some new properties are built. The first step is to clear the land and then dig a trench for the drainage facilities. It's easy to dig the trench to the legal depth and then install the sewage pipes directly into the trench. These should be surrounded by hard core and sand but once the trench has been filled in nobody will see that this has not been done. We actually saw a new main sewer for 250 apartments being laid in a regulation-depth trench with no support whatsoever and this was in an area which has the potential for earthquake activity.

The next stage is to lay the foundations. This is usually a concrete platform which really should be laid on well prepared soil with a good damp-proof membrane under the concrete. This does not always happen. The concrete is often just poured onto the levelled soil followed by the installation of the concrete pillars which are filled in with breeze blocks to form the walls. On occasions these walls are only one block thick – even between adjacent townhouses or apartments. Staircases are concrete poured into a wooden framework but once the wood has been removed and the staircase is clad in marble it will look wonderful.

Many of the new properties on the coast are really only built as holiday homes with insulation and sound deadening to match. They are not always built as properties in which anyone would want to live all year round.

Once finished many of these properties look wonderful but there is virtually no way that you can check the build quality. High quality kitchens and gold plated taps in the bathroom can be very seductive but they are not expensive in Spain and do help to seduce buyers into buying a new property.

Unlike in the UK, structural surveys are not an automatic part of the buying process. However, structural surveyors do exist and it's worth having a survey, particularly if your chosen property is an older property or has been renovated. Many people simply ask a builder to have a look at the property and report on how it has been built. I would always recommend the purchase of a resale property because at least you can check on build quality by talking to existing neighbours.

Q 'Do all the necessary facilities exist and if not, can they be installed?'

Many inland properties aren't connected to a water supply and may have to rely on a private well. Check that the well produces sufficient water for all year round living. Is the water drinking quality? This can be checked by your local water authority.

Electricity can also be a problem. We viewed one property which was only 30 kilometres inland from the coast which did have mains electricity, but it was a spur from the cables which passed over the mountainside next to the property - it might have been legal but I suspect it was not. If there is electricity in the near vicinity it should be possible to connect to the mains supply but otherwise you will be dependent on generators or solar electricity. This means that all your electrical appliances will have to operate on a 12 volt system. Solar power, if you can harness enough, is a good alternative in Spanish coastal areas which have a lot of sun. We have friends who power most of their hot water and heating from solar panels, not just for their own house but also for a four-bedroom guest house, although it can still have some inconveniences.

Telephone and internet connections are another potential problem. In some rural areas the installation of a landline is virtually impossible because there are no cables in place. You might have to rely on a satellite telephone system or your mobile telephone and there is often a poor reception in rural areas. This can be a problem if you want to work from your new home, especially if you also need a fast broadband connection to the Internet. Once more you really need to do your own homework and not just listen to the local estate agent who might tell you exactly what you want to hear.

If you really need broadband and the house already has a telephone, it should be possible but you must check out the availability of broadband, usually with *Telefónica*, before you make an offer. If the house does not have a telephone, assume that broadband might not be available for a long time to come.

Drainage and sanitation are not usually a great problem as long as there is a good water supply. In many parts of Europe, rural locations can be a long distance from the nearest town sanitation systems but it's very easy to install septic tanks and soak-aways which will provide you with a sanitation system which is just as good as any you would find in an urban environment. However, a completely new sanitation system isn't cheap and could cost several thousand euros. If there is already a septic tank at the property, you should get it thoroughly checked and make sure it meets national and EU regulations.

There are now so many EU laws which govern how such systems should be installed and you should get professional advice because the regulations are changing all the time. If the property already has a septic tank system it may not need to be inspected under EU regulations but if it is a new renovation you will be faced with the current regulations, inspections and approvals.

Q **'Does the property and land come with the necessary planning permission for my proposed renovations or development?'**

This was a route favoured by many people in the past; buy a ruin in the country, demolish it and rebuild a wonderful new house three times the size of the ruin. However, planning rules have been tightened up and in many parts of Spain you can still demolish but the new property must have the same floor area of the property which was demolished. So if you buy a 100 square metre house you can only replace it with a house of the same size.

If you decide to buy a plot of land deep in the Spanish countryside on which you plan to build your dream home you really need to visit the local Town Hall with your lawyer and preferably an architect with plans for your proposed property. You must do this before you sign any documents, otherwise you could end up owning a beautiful piece of Spanish countryside but unable to do anything with it. Don't listen to the seller who tries to tell you that you can buy the land, build a house illegally and then have it officially registered after the event. This used to happen but laws have been tightened up and it is impossible to do that now.

Most country plots are designated as *rústico*, this means that they are not designated for development but are classified as pasture, farmland or forest. This classification applies to about 75 per cent of the total land mass in Spain. Development on this type of land is severely restricted and the restrictions vary according to where you buy. In general, building permission may be granted but the minimum plot size is usually 3,000 square metres of land and may be as high as 10,000 or even 15,000 square metres in some regions and must usually have a water source. There are also restrictions on the type of building that is allowed in some regions. It's vital to check with the Town Hall before you commit yourself to a plot of land, wherever it is.

For example, in 2002, the regional government of Andalusia passed new laws to prevent the area's beautiful countryside being spoilt by the same levels of development that have afflicted much of its coastline. The new law has made it very difficult, if not impossible to build on a *parcela rústica* (rural plot) unless your proposed building meets stringent criteria.

Even if you love the idea of living in remote countryside, remember that you can't live without a water source to meet your basic needs. You can't cook, install a septic tank or irrigate your land should you want to be self-sufficient. Living with electricity is more feasible thanks to solar power and there are always petrol-driven generators to provide electricity. Contact with the outside world can be via your mobile telephone, which can always be recharged through your electricity source, and internet access is available via satellite. Remember that this may be necessary even 5–10 kilometres inland from the coastal areas.

You also need to check that any land you purchase does not have a public right of way across it. This could become a road or even a motorway in the future.

Whatever land you buy in the country areas, ask your lawyer to consult a land surveyor who will draw up an accurate plan of the land you are purchasing, it is not good enough for the seller to say that the land 'ends at that line of trees over there'. The land needs to be mapped out and, if possible, have some sort of boundary fence put around it. Your lawyer must thoroughly investigate the status of the land and the conditions and regulations which may affect your intended use of it.

'Will I have problems accessing the property in winter?'

Many people searching for a property tend to view a prospective purchase in the spring, summer or early autumn. At these times of year, dirt-track access to some of the more remote Spanish properties can be quite charmingly rustic. This might not be the case when the first rains of late autumn arrive and the dirt-track turns into a mud track or access becomes difficult, or even possible, during the first snow of winter.

We viewed one property which definitely fell into this category. It was a small inland *finca* at the end of a very steep dirt-track. Parts of the dirt-track had a sheer rock face on one side and a precipitous drop on the other. There was neither parapet nor crash barriers and the track was only wide enough for one car. We travelled with the estate agent who followed the owner, who was driving a 4 x 4, to the property car. At one point the estate agent actually stopped where there was room to turn and said that he could not possibly go any further because his car was bottoming out on the track. We walked the rest of the way to the property through the garden which was a wild herb meadow with amazing scents. You could 'hear' the silence, broken only by the sound of birdsong and cow bells on the neighbouring hillsides. It was a beautiful location with breathtaking views but it was clear that access was virtually impossible even in the early autumn. It was rejected.

We viewed another inland property, a new build country house which, when finished would be wonderful and the price was right. However, access was up a mountain track in the estate agent's 4 x 4. Sitting high up in the vehicle bouncing along this track with a view straight down into the valley and no visibility of the edge of the road was enough for me. I was completely unnerved by the journey and when we arrived at the house I actually did not want to see it. The views were magnificent. The house was very attractive but I would not have wanted to drive up or down that track every time I went out and I doubt if many friends would have wanted to visit – they would certainly not have visited in the dark.

Many books have been written which describe the idyllic return to nature of many Brits in the past. However, I ask readers to seriously ask themselves whether they would really like to live in an area which is so remote. It is one thing to read about it and dream, but a totally different experience if you have to live with it every day. If access is difficult, you should also consider how your personal belongings will actually get to your remote idyll, How will a large removal van gain access? What if you buy a large item locally? How will it be delivered?

 ## 'Does the property fulfil all legal requirements?'

This is something which your Spanish lawyer must investigate in detail. In many parts of Spain, both coastal and inland regions, there are *parcelas* (plots) of land which legally belong to an individual or individuals. However, a house may have been built on the land without planning permission. Whatever type of Spanish property you buy and wherever it is, you must make sure that it is totally legal. If you don't do this, however innocently, you will end up being the one who pays the price in more ways than one. It will not be the estate agent or the lawyer or the town hall official.

We have a good and honest estate agent who has driven us past many beautiful inland properties and said 'This is a beautiful house and it is for sale but it was built illegally. In law, it does not exist, so don't even look at it.' However, if you use an estate agent who is perhaps not as honest as ours, it may be a different story. With one eye on commission and the fact that you might never see them again, you may find that the agent conveniently knows a local lawyer who will be prepared to bend the rules and who will 'act' on your behalf. If you follow this route because you have fallen in love with the property it could all backfire on you. You could find yourself being the owner of a property which does not exist in law. If the Spanish authorities decide that the new motorway, which is vital to the local economy and to local development, will pass directly across your house, they usually show little sympathy for illegal properties which stand in the way. If you are lucky, they might pay compensation for the value of your land, but that is all.

We know of people who were trapped in this way, in a non-legal house on 25,000 square metres of land. The local authorities paid them the equivalent of fifty pence per square metre for the land so that a motorway viaduct could be built across their valley. They had no legal leg to stand on when they lost their house because in law their house did not actually exist. So they received just £12,500!

'What is the Valencia Land Grab?'

The possibility of having your land literally 'grabbed' off you in Valencia has been widely, and sometimes sensationally, highlighted in the British media over the last few years. It refers to a highly controversial law and the way it has been enforced with some people losing land which they considered belonged to them. As a result, some politicians at the European level have become involved and an end to the problem appears to be in sight, but what does the law actually mean and who could be affected?

In any country there is land which is already urbanised, land which could be urbanised and land which is rural. As the demand for new property increases, local authorities sometimes have to take the difficult decision to re-classify land as suitable for development. The infamous Valencia Land Grab dispute arose out of a law introduced in Valencia to promote urban development so that they could build low-cost housing and improve public services. Many local landowners refused to participate in the development projects and so the *Ley Reguladora de Actividad Urbanística/LRAU* (The Urban Development Legislation) came into force in 1994. The *LRAU* meant that landowners had to be part of any development project approved by the Town Hall and pay towards the infrastructure which would ultimately benefit them.

Initially the *LRAU* worked well and some areas benefited considerably by the new development and public services. However, the Valencian region also includes the popular coastal areas of the Costa Blanca and the Costa del Azahar and, with undeveloped land in these areas at a premium the *LRAU* was abused by some developers and corrupt local authorities. The law had been badly drafted and allowed developers to buy what was originally rural land – at way below the market value for land – develop it, and make a huge profit. Under the auspices of the *LRAU*, ordinary property owners were treated like the landowners and made to sell their property and contribute to the infrastructure of the new development. The developers demanded payment from the existing owners for the 'urbanisation' of the land, which many owners did not want, preferring to live in their old rural ways.

Unfortunately, many of the owners don't live in their properties all year round and the authorities were only required to give 15 days notice of the expropriation of their land. After a period away from their house they returned to find the developers had actually moved in with their bulldozers and they also had a bill from the Town Hall requesting payment for the changes which were being made. Hence the 'shock-horror' articles in the British media. Many depicted it as an anti-British campaign, although Spaniards and many other nationalities faced the same problems as British owners. One more reason why your lawyer should check everything before you sign any document. Is the land approved for building? Is the specific house that you want to build approved for this land?

The law is really no different from a compulsory purchase order on property in the UK which has been made so that something else can be built which will benefit the local community. The only difference in Valencia was that the property owner was also expected to pay towards these benefits. This is a bit like discovering that your land has a compulsory purchase order on it because the local authority needs to build a second runway at your local airport. Except that not only might you get a derisory price for the land but you also have to pay the costs of installing the runway on your own land. The compulsory purchase might be acceptable at the right price but to be asked to pay for the development is unacceptable and that has been the real problem.

Because of the involvement of the European Parliament and its criticism of the misuse of the LRAU, a new law, known as the *Ley Urbanística Valenciana/LAU* (Valencian Urban Law) recently came into force and which should protect the rights of property owners in the future. Some of the owners who have been affected may receive compensation. Check with your lawyer about the new law. It is worth remembering that this problem has only really affected a very small number of property buyers in Spain and only affects property on undeveloped land within the autonomous community of Valencia.

If you buy a property in Spain which has been built on land classified as urban and therefore available for development, and you use the services of a good Spanish lawyer you should have no problems. However, you should always avoid rural properties with dubious planning permission wherever they are, in Valencia or anywhere else in Spain.

'Does the property or development have full planning permission?'

In the last chapter I dealt with possible problems concerning illegally built country properties, but illegal properties don't just exist in rural areas. It can also happen on the coast and indeed has happened in several highly publicised cases over the last few years. Corrupt local authorities have accepted bribes of hundreds of thousands of euros to grant illegal planning permission for properties which should not have been built.

You are not immune from these problems even if you are very well-known and have plenty of money. Antonio Banderas, the famous actor and film star, bought an expensive villa in Marbella and discovered later that the house was illegal and he was faced with a demolition order. The final outcome of his case has not yet been decided and at the time of writing the house still stands. Many people think that because he is such a high profile personality – along with Picasso he is known as one of Malaga's favourite sons – an exception will be made in his case.

We have lived in an urbanisation which had a *plan parcial* dating from the 1980s for planned development over a period of many years. There was planning permission for villas, some apartments and a large green space which was supposed to be maintained. Without warning, it was decided that the green space would be used for hundreds of apartments. There was no planning permission, they were officially illegal and could be demolished at any time. The community of owners created a website warning potential buyers not to buy in this development because some of the new properties were illegal and could face a demolition order. If you try to look up this website you will find that access is now denied. Yet access is not denied to the websites of the many agents who are now selling these 'illegal' properties. Many of these agents are British and the property descriptions sound wonderful and they are still on the market.

'How could illegal planning permission affect me in the future?'

It is difficult to give a definitive answer to this question. If your development is illegal, it could, in theory, be subject to a demolition order, even if you think you're the innocent party. I have already described the new apartments on the top of the hill behind our property, which are strictly speaking illegal although people are still buying them and the agents are still showing them. They could, in theory, face a demolition order at any time.

There have been some highly publicised demolitions recently, primarily of properties built in contravention of the *Ley de Costas* and there are many more threatened as a result of the Marbella Town Hall corruption scandal of 2006. Even if planning permission has been granted, it may have been granted by a corrupt town hall official and may be withdrawn at a later date.

However, the new Mayor of Marbella, who represents a political party which isn't associated with any corruption, has publicly stated that there are now so many illegal properties around Marbella she will have to grant an amnesty and back-dated planning permission. Otherwise the lives of so many people who have invested in these properties could be ruined.

'How successful will it be as a rental investment – what income should I expect?'

If you're buying as an investment you need to be able to generate at least a 5 per cent return on the money you pay for the property – after all you can get this return from a carefully chosen bank account. Therefore if you buy for €200,000 you need a return of €10,000 per year. If you hope to let your property for 20 weeks of the year, the average rent has to be €500 every week. Before you commit yourself to any purchase check out the kind of rents you can charge in your chosen area and how many properties are available for holiday lets. Then consider whether your chosen property could attract that kind of rent.

So many holiday visitors have become property owners and as a consequence there are now far more properties available than there are potential tenants. As a result many buyers are becoming very disappointed or even desperate if they have to pay a mortgage on the property which their estate agent told them they would be able to let out for 20 weeks a year. No estate agent can tell you this and look you straight in the eye and presenters on the TV property programmes should be banned from saying, 'and of course when you are not here you could get £500 a week for this property', it's just not true!

'Have all the bills been paid on my property or are there outstanding debts?'

This is a very important question which your lawyer must thoroughly investigate. When you buy a property in Spain you also buy any unpaid bills or charges, such as mortgages, which might be attached to that property. If the previous owner did not pay the electricity bill or local taxes, they become your responsibility. If the mortgage is in arrears, it becomes your mortgage. This is something which a good lawyer, experienced in Spanish property conveyance, will check before anything else.

We have a friend who returned home to find that her electricity had been disconnected. Unbeknown to her, there was an unpaid (or underpaid) bill for €8 owed to the electricity company. Their first step, without any warning, was to disconnect the supply and she had to go to the electricity company's office and pay the amount owing plus a reconnection charge.

Other acquaintances bought a bar in one of the Balearic Islands. They rushed the purchase through because they were desperate to own the bar and they did not take full legal advice. They found out later that the electricity, telephone and other suppliers' bills had been outstanding for some time and there was a huge burden of debt on the property, including an unpaid mortgage. This debt almost resulted in them being declared bankrupt because they had overstretched themselves in the first place to buy the bar and did not have the cash to pay either the outstanding bills or the mortgage. They were unable to open for business because all the services had been disconnected. It is part of your lawyer's job to check this, so make sure you commission the services of a lawyer who is looking after your interests.

'What are urbanisation charges and what do they cover?'

This will vary depending on what has been agreed by the community of owners. Usually these charges cover things like the landscaping and maintenance of communal garden areas, exterior painting of apartment blocks on a regular basis, maintenance of communal swimming pools, insurance of the structure of any apartment blocks, maintenance of the access roads if the local Town Hall has not taken them over and maintenance of essential services. The charges are paid by each owner and usually depend on the habitable floor space of your property.

Some estate agents do not even tell prospective purchasers that these annual charges exist, but any good lawyer should check your obligations. Remember that if you move into an urbanisation you will always have to pay these charges, although the amounts and what you pay for differ from one urbanisation to another. You will not be able to claim that you did not know about them and refuse to pay. You're legally obliged to pay these charges annually and you have no alternative. The President of the community has legal powers under Spanish law and, after a period of non-payment and several warning letters, your property could legally be auctioned by the community so that they can recover any unpaid annual charges.

If you wish to sell your property and there are outstanding community fees, the community can withhold the necessary documents for the sale to proceed. Many sellers have been caught out and find that when they want to sell they have to pay all outstanding charges for the previous five years. You can ask the agent about community fees and what they cover, but your lawyer should check the details and confirm it to you.

We live in a community where the President takes a tough line and takes owners to court for non-payment of community charges. As a result our community has been well looked after and continues to be well maintained because almost everyone pays. However, there are many urbanisations which look shabby and are badly maintained because these communities are unable to collect all the fees.

As these developments become more and more dilapidated everyone loses out and the value of your investment immediately drops. If you buy a property in an urbanisation, ask your lawyer to ensure that all the residents pay their charges on a regular basis as this will be in your own long-term interests.

 ## Summary

- Look carefully at the questions in this chapter before you commit yourself to the purchase of any Spanish property. Don't let your dreams take over – be realistic.

- Make sure that your lawyer checks that your chosen property is legally built and cannot be threatened in the future.

- Make sure that there are no outstanding bills attached to the property.

- If you intend to let your property, check that the potential income will cover your financial commitments.

- Check also what the running costs of the property might be.

Glossary

urbanización	an urbanisation. A development of apartments, townhouses or villas.
plan parcial	the local municipal plan for the area which shows that the land that your property is built on was approved for development.
denuncia	an official complaint or reporting of a crime to the police.
parcela rústico	rural plot.

Chapter 6
How much will the property really cost?

When you buy a property in Spain, you should budget for at least an extra 10 per cent on the price to cover taxes and legal fees which are involved. You also need to take into consideration what the running costs will be. Aside from your mortgage payments there are local taxes, community fees if you live on an urbanisation, utility bills and, if necessary, the costs of redecoration or modernisation. It's important to remember these extra costs if you are working to a tight budget. I would suggest that you add 15 per cent to the asking price to cover your costs for the first year plus the mortgage repayments if you have one. If you're planning to buy for investment reasons, then you should check that your rental returns will cover these additional costs.

'What's included in the price?'

Normally the sales price includes the estate agent fees. So although, in theory, the vendor pays these, effectively the buyer does. If the property is to be sold furnished, which is fairly common, you should ensure that an inventory of the furnishings and fittings is included in the contract. You also need to check that all listed items are actually left in the property. If possible, you should check this a few hours before the sale is closed. Anything which is to be left in the property should be included in the contract.

'Should I try to negotiate a cash payment?'

You should be very careful about cash payments, however innocent. As explained below, the Spanish government has recently introduced tough laws to combat money-laundering through property purchase. However, it may be possible to negotiate a reasonable cash payment for the fixtures and fittings. Although this is legal, it's getting more difficult to do and you should always take the advice of your lawyer. If you're able to do this it could reduce your tax liability.

The first property we sold had an agreed cash payment for fixtures and fittings which had been organised by the estate agent. On the day of completion everyone arrived at the notary's office including the bank. The agent had a cheque from the bank for the official transfer of the mortgage funds and an envelope with the cash payment of €20,000 in €500 notes which was passed to us when the notary had temporarily left the room. This was because he did not want to officially see the cash crossing the table. The only problem we then had was that we could not pay this money into our account in total because any payment of more than €6,000 per day has to be declared to the *Banco de España* (Bank of Spain) - a law introduced to prevent money-laundering. So it took four days to pay all the money into our account.

This kind of thing happened regularly just a few years ago but these days you will find that lawyers and notaries are far less willing to turn a blind eye and all payments and their sources must be noted on the *escritura*. The government's tough new stance means that lawyers and notaries have a lot to lose if they appear to have been involved in these practices.

 ### 'How does the 'black' economy work in property transactions?'

In theory, it doesn't any more. However, you may find that the vendor of your property asks for a certain amount of the sale price in cash. Under-declaration used to be rife in Spain, although the practice is illegal under both Spanish and EU law. However, as explained above, the Spanish government have recently cracked down on the practice and I would strongly advise against it. The reason for under-declaration is that the lower the declared price, the less profit the seller appears to have made. This helps to lower the Capital Gains Tax (CGT) liability. The buyer is also required to pay property transfer tax which is 7 per cent of the purchase price so it could be in the buyer's interest to accept an under-declaration to reduce the tax bill at the time of the purchase.

The second time we almost became involved in this type of transaction was when we found our ideal country property. The price of the house was €300,000. This was right at the top end of our budget and would have left us with very little cash in the bank. When we told the estate agent that we would like to start negotiations, the vendor said that she wanted the price recorded as €100,000 on the official documents and this was non-negotiable. We walked away from this purchase. There was no way that we would have agreed to only a third of the price being declared on the title deeds. That could have been storing up real problems for our future because when we came to sell, it would appear that we had made a far greater profit than we actually had. We would have been the ones to pay the tax on that so-called profit.

The local tax office may intervene if the declared value of the property is less than roughly twice the *valor catastral* (the rateable value) of the property. The *valor catastral* is well below the actual sales price and can be found on the receipts for local taxes (known as the *IBI*) which your lawyer should have checked on your behalf.

If the tax authorities decide that the house has been under-valued, they can impose a surcharge of 6 per cent on the difference. If the value is heavily under-declared, by 20 per cent less, the buyer can be taxed on the difference as if it was a gift from the seller. We know people who have had such tax demands and they have had to pay them.

'Should I get involved in cash transactions in property purchase?'

In one word - no. It's illegal and the Spanish authorities have made it virtually impossible to get involved in cash transactions. Your Spanish lawyer should be aware of this and advise you accordingly. If the seller does not agree to this then walk away from the purchase. Bite the bullet and pay the initial taxes because you will benefit in the long term.

Q 'What taxes will be incurred as a result of buying this property?'

Depending on whether it is a new or resale property, the buyer must pay what is known as *Impuesto de Transmisiones Patrimoniales/ITP* (transfer tax) on a resale property or *Impuesto sobre el Valor Añadido/IVA*, which is Spanish VAT, on a new property. The *ITP* is payable on the transfer of the resale property and varies from region to region but is around 7 per cent. *IVA* is currently 7 per cent for property purchases across the country.

You should also ask the estate agent and your lawyer to find out about annual local taxes. They are known as *Impuesto sobre Bienes Inmuebles/IBI* and are usually less than council tax or what we used to know as the rates in the UK. Your lawyer should ask for copies of the previous year's bills and proof that they have been paid. Local taxes vary according to the region in which you are buying. They will be at their highest in highly developed cities and towns and relatively low in more rural areas.

Taxes such as the *IBI* should be paid within 30 days at the local town hall and your lawyer can arrange this but if you manage to escape the taxman for five years you will not have to pay anything. The Spanish tax authorities can only back-date tax for five years although they are tightening up on the regulations.

'How much property owner's income tax will I have to pay?'

If you're a resident, you only pay this tax on a second home. If you are a non-resident you pay it on all property in Spain and declare it along with any other income you may have in Spain. The non-resident's property tax is an imputed letting tax (or income tax on letting income) and is charged at 2 per cent of the *valor catastral*. This tax assumes that if you're non-resident then you must be letting the property and the Spanish government wants their cut of any possible income - even if you're not actually letting it.

If you're a resident for tax purposes and have a second property in Spain, whatever your nationality, you will be liable for this tax on your second property and this will be added to your annual income tax bill. The property must be accounted for on your annual tax return.

'What is wealth tax, and will I have to pay it on this property?'

This tax is often referred to as the *Patrimonio* but its full name is *Impuesto Extraordinario sobre El Patrimonio* (literally, an extraordinary tax on assets). A resident will pay this tax on all their assets; property, bank deposits, stocks and shares, cars, boats or indeed anything which could be described as wealth. Residents have to declare the value of their worldwide assets every year and they then qualify for an initial deduction if their property is a principal residence, before the taxable amount is calculated. Rates vary according to the value of the property and are between 0.2 and 2.5 per cent. Non-residents should pay this tax on the total value of their assets in Spain, including property. Rates are the same but non-residents are not entitled to any deductions. Your tax representative (see the next paragraph) or your *gestor* (see later) can advise you on this tax.

If you own more than one property or other assets in Spain, you are required by law to appoint an official *representante fiscal* (tax representative). If you fail to do so you could be liable to a fine of up to €6,000. The Spanish tax authorities need to know that they have a reliable authority in Spain to deal with your tax liabilities. Your estate agent may know a good fiscal adviser or, if you have appointed a *gestor*, he will certainly be able to make a recommendation.

If you are a non-resident and only own one property, it's no longer a legal requirement to appoint a fiscal representative, but I would recommend that you do so. They can look after all your Spanish financial affairs, pay taxes on your behalf and communicate with the tax authorities. Their fees are generally reasonable and it's definitely worth it for the peace of mind.

'How much local tax will I have to pay? '

This tax, the *IBI*, was described earlier when I explained that you should ensure it has been paid up to the date of completion of the sale. This is the Spanish equivalent of council tax and varies, depending on where you live. It could be less than €100 per year for a country property or a few thousand for a well-positioned villa in somewhere like Marbella. This tax rises automatically every year in line with inflation. The best way of paying this tax is by direct debit from your Spanish bank account, particularly if you're a non-resident.

Property owners' taxes vary depending on whether you're a resident or non-resident, but everyone must pay *IBI*, the local tax and the *Patrimonio*, although rates differ depending on your residency status. Non-residents also pay an imputed letting tax. It's impossible to generalise about the amount of tax you will have to pay and so it's essential to get advice on your own situation from a qualified tax adviser. In addition, if you have bought in an urbanisation you will also have community fees to pay and this could add a considerable amount to your annual bills.

Don't think that you will get away with ignoring these taxes, as soon as you have an *NIE* number, which you must have for any major financial transactions in Spain, the tax authorities can track your liabilities. When you come to sell your property, the notary is entitled to retain 3 per cent of the sales price to cover any unpaid taxes.

If you're buying property in Spain, it's important to consider not just the initial buying costs but also running costs, whether you live there permanently or on a part-time basis. You need to build this into your future budget. If you're planning to let your property, you must build these costs into your rental rates. More than €250 per month may be already earmarked for the taxman, maintenance costs and the urbanisation charges.

 ### 'Will my heirs have to pay inheritance tax? '

Many people who move to Spain and buy property there completely ignore or do not even consider the question of Inheritance Tax. You won't ever have to pay this tax, but your beneficiaries will so it's vital to find out what their liability might be or they could find themselves with a large tax bill. The rules differ quite considerably from those in the UK and there is no total exemption between official partners, although there are ways in which liability can be minimised and you should consult your financial adviser or lawyer as soon as you have assets in Spain. There are exemptions depending on the relationship between the deceased and the beneficiary, but there is no exemption at all if property is left to a non-related beneficiary. Those who have been officially resident in Spain for at least three years can get substantial tax breaks but the beneficiary must have been living with the donor for at least two years and must not sell the property for ten years. You must take advice from a lawyer about your personal situation.

This is not a tax which you will ever have to pay but it could be important to your family or friends.

Q 'What costs are involved in the process of buying the house?'

As described earlier you should add at least 10 per cent of the agreed purchase price to allow for the costs involved in the purchase procedure in Spain. This is higher than the costs involved in buying in many other countries and many buyers have been surprised or caught out because they have not done their homework. Many do not even think that there will be additional costs. If you buy at an agreed price of €200,000, you should budget for at least €220,000.

The additional costs cover national and local taxes incurred when buying and transferring property as well as legal fees and notary costs. You also need to ensure that you agree through your lawyer and the seller about who pays what, Spanish law leaves the buyer and vendor considerable leeway to agree the terms on which the transaction takes place. This can and should be written into the initial contract - one more reason why you need an experienced English-speaking Spanish lawyer who understands the system.

Fees are generally the responsibility of the person who contracts the services, therefore the vendor should be responsible for the commission payable to the estate agent, although in practice, it's often simply added to the sale price. As the buyer, you will be responsible for your lawyer's fees which are between 1 and 2 per cent of the property's value, and the fees of any surveyor or builder who inspects the property on your behalf. You will also be responsible for the payment of the *Impuesto de Transmisiones Patrimoniales* (*ITP*), which is a transfer tax or in the case of a new property the *IVA* (VAT), plus stamp duty and a fee for registration of the new title deeds in the land registry. In addition, you will have to pay the fees for the *notario* and the *gestor* (if you use them).

You may also have to build in translation costs for any official documents you have to sign. It's vital that you understand everything before you sign it. You will incur no extra charges for paying in cash but if you are buying with a mortgage you should allow around 1.5 per cent for the mortgage set-up fee.

The vendor will also be responsible for several taxes which must be paid unless agreed otherwise. One thing which you or your lawyer must not agree to on the sales contract is that you, the buyer, is responsible for *todos los gastos* – if you agree to this then you will be responsible for all the costs involved in selling and buying and the seller will pay nothing. This is when it pays to have a truly independent lawyer, if, for example, the lawyer acting for you is also working for an unscrupulous developer, the lawyer could try to write this into the contract without you realising so that the developer escapes any costs.

'How much will the equivalent of stamp duty be?'

The buyer is also responsible for the Spanish equivalent of stamp duty, known as *Impuesto sobre Actos Jurídicos Documentados (AJD)*, which is the legal document fee and is between 0.5 and 1 per cent of the declared value, depending on the region. *AJD* is only payable on new properties being sold for the first time. With a resale property, it's included in the transfer tax. To be fair to the Spanish authorities, while some taxes are higher than they are in the UK, stamp duty is much lower on expensive properties because it's a fixed percentage, no matter what the value of the property.

'What does the vendor normally pay for?'

Officially, the vendor pays the estate agent's commission, although this is often included in the original asking price. Estate agent's commission can be a tricky problem, it's usually 5 per cent, but is often negotiable and can be much higher, sometimes up to 10 per cent. This expenditure can be offset against Capital Gains Tax if you have a receipt to show you have paid it. On one occasion when we had sold a property, I asked the agent for a receipt only to be told that I would have to pay 16 per cent *IVA* on the fee before they would issue a receipt. This agent, a highly regarded local business, was obviously not declaring *IVA* on every transaction. Your lawyer should ensure that the vendor pays the costs of cancelling any mortgage which already exists on the property and pays all outstanding taxes and bills associated with the property up to the date of transfer. If there is a mortgage on the property and it is not cancelled, you could be buying a property and the vendor's mortgage!

Your lawyer should ask for receipts for all payments made, including *IBI* payments, all outstanding utility bills up to the date of completion and community charges on any property in an urbanisation. Some urbanisations are run so well that permission to sell will not be given unless all payments are up to date.

The other tax, a local land tax, which is normally paid by the vendor is referred to as the *plus valía* in short, its full name is *Impuesto Municipal sobre el Incremento de Valor de los Terrenos* - quite a mouthful, which is why it is shortened! This is a tax imposed on the increased value of the land since it was last sold. You should be able to find out how much it will be on your property by asking at the local tax office. Normally the vendor is responsible but you should confirm this and have it written into the contract.

Some developers insist that buyers pay this tax and we had an argument with the developers of the first apartment on which we made an offer – they insisted that we should be responsible for payment. Our lawyer argued that they should be responsible since they had developed the land and they were the ones making a profit on the development so why should we pay? Our lawyer won – so it's worth fighting.

If you buy an apartment or a townhouse in an urbanisation, there may not be a significant increase in the value of the land since it was last sold. However, if you buy a country property standing in a large amount of land, the *plus valía* could be very high, especially if it has been re-classified as urban land since the last sale. Urban land is worth far more than rural land. Depending on where your property is and the number of the years that the vendor has owned it, this tax can be fairly high and is not related to the value of the property. Therefore you should not agree to be responsible for payment until you have checked what amount might have to be paid with the local tax office. For example, we have friends who bought a country property for renovation about 12 years ago. At that time it was in the middle of nowhere with only a dirt-track access road and no mains sanitation. Now it's surrounded by new villas and townhouses so the local land, including their property, has obviously been re-classified as an urban area and has modern services and an established infrastructure. As a result the value of their land is likely to have increased dramatically, which is wonderful for them if they decide to sell. However, it could be a nightmare for any buyer who may have to pay the *plus valia* if these owners don't agree to pay the tax or conveniently *forget* to pay and then disappear. This has happened when non-resident vendors return to their country of origin - without leaving a forwarding address – the buyer ends up paying.

The simplest way to avoid this tax as a buyer is to agree in the contract that the estimated tax liability will be deducted from the purchase price and held by the *notario*. As previously discussed, you or your lawyer can visit the local tax office and find out the likely amount of tax and you then negotiate accordingly. This is particularly important if the estimated *plus valia* is a sizeable sum.

 'What would a hypothetical purchase cost?'

For an apartment on the Costa del Sol with a purchase price of €200,000 (full declared price):

Transfer tax (*ITP*) or VAT (*IVA*) at 7 per cent	14,000
Lawyer's fees at 1 per cent (approx.)	2,000
Notary fees, gestor and registry fees (estimate)	2,000
Stamp duty at 1 per cent	2,000
Total	€20,000

To this sum you may have to add the *plus valía* if you have agreed to pay it. Factoring in these costs would take the purchase costs to at least 10 per cent. You will also have to pay *IVA* on your legal and estate agent's bills at 16 per cent.

'What is the current state of the property?'

Initially only you can decide this. Does it need to be redecorated? Does it appear to need major renovation work? Could I move in and live in the property today?

If the property is in the country and requires total renovation then, before you complete the purchase, you need to ensure that you have accurate and realistic estimates of any planned renovation costs – not just the hypothetical figure guessed by an estate agent during the sales pitch. Estate agents always underestimate the costs of renovation or simply pluck a figure from the air. You must consult an architect or a builder before you commit yourself and then add a contingency figure. I have never known a renovation to come in on budget.

If the property is more modern you may still have to budget for things like re-wiring, re-plumbing, installation of a new kitchen or bathroom(s), or perhaps even more extensive work and if you have overstretched yourself in the first place, this could cause you long-term financial problems. Many relatively new properties will probably require some renovation, and this must be factored into the costs of buying. Build quality in Spain 20-30 years ago was not always of the highest standard.

'What is the state of the roof?'

In relatively new coastal properties this question is irrelevant because the roof is likely to be concrete covered with terracotta tiles to make the property look authentic. The concrete stops the water coming in and the tiles are decorative. In country properties the state of the roof could be more important. If it appears to be sagging you should call in a builder to give an opinion. If there is no sign of

141

water damage in the rooms below the roof you're probably OK.

'How much might it cost to put right any problems with the roof?'

This depends on where you live. In the wealthy tourist areas builders often try to charge whatever they think you might pay. Bear in mind that there are unlikely to be major problems in modern properties. In rural areas you need to find a good local builder who would do the necessary work of re-tiling a roof on a wood base. The good thing about terracotta roof tiles in Spain is that they are much cheaper than in many other countries.

'What state are the walls in?'

New properties are likely to be constructed of concrete and there should be no problems with the state of the walls. In central and northern Spain old properties are usually built in stone and the walls will be around 2 feet thick. They have probably been there for several hundred years, and there is really nothing you need to do to check them. If you bring in a surveyor from the UK he will almost certainly point out the lack of a damp-course. However, it's important to remember that these old houses were not built with damp-courses and there is almost no way that they can be installed now. No-one asks whether Windsor Castle has a damp-course!

'Has the property been treated for insect infestation?'

This is sometimes a problem in Spain and there is woodworm and termite activity in some areas, which can be difficult to detect unless it's really extensive. If the property is an older property it would be wise to ask your lawyer for proof that it has been checked for infestation. Although there is no legal requirement for an official certificate to say that the property is free of insect activity, if I were buying an older property I would ask for one and when I moved in, have the wood treated against future infestation.

'When was the property last re-wired or re-plumbed and does everything work properly?'

In a relatively new property this is an academic question and you should not need to get involved in re-wiring or re-plumbing. In a property 20-30 years old you should ask a local electrician or plumber to have a look at the current installation. Your lawyer should be able to provide contacts. The costs of re-wiring will depend on where you live, the size of the house, how much work is required and whether you choose to use an electrician from the UK or a local Spanish electrician. Not only is a Spanish electrician likely to be much cheaper, but more importantly, he will also be properly qualified with the correct licences which are required by law. The cost of new plumbing for bathrooms or kitchens will be much lower than the equivalent in the UK but of course the price depends on the kind of fittings you choose.

'How much might it cost to install a swimming pool?'

An 8 x 4 metre swimming pool would cost around €20,000 for a basic installation of a liner pool plus pool equipment. A concrete tiled pool will of course be more expensive. You will need to apply for planning permission from the Town Hall and, if you are in an urbanisation, from the committee representing the community of owners. Many new expensive villas will already include a swimming pool but if you buy a small villa on an urbanisation you will probably have to install your own pool, it is then up to you to decide how much of the garden you can give up. The authorities can be very strict on the safety and may insist that your pool needs to be fenced in according to current EU laws.

'How much of the necessary work am I capable of doing myself and how much time do I have to do it?'

This depends totally on your DIY skills and how much work you are capable of taking on. Many people love DIY and the challenge of creating their new home but to do this you need time so make sure you consider this before you buy a property that needs extensive renovation. If you don't have the time to do the work yourself, can you afford to employ tradesmen? If you have the skills and the time you will be pleasantly surprised by the low cost of building materials in Spain.

'What is the energy rating of the property?'

Spanish property is not yet rated in the same way that UK property is in the new Home Information Packs (HIPS). If you ask a Spanish estate agent this question you are likely to receive a totally blank response. I have seen a lot of new buildings under construction in the south of Spain, but very little evidence of significant amounts of insulation being installed and many are not even double-glazed. Of course, the climate is generally warmer than northern Europe. In an area where the power of the sun is considerable, very little is harnessed for solar power. Older properties in inland areas built of stone are likely to be better insulated simply because of the thickness of the walls.

'How is the property heated?'

In coastal areas there will probably be no heating provision apart from a log-burner and electrical power points. Logs are cheap and you can boost the heating with electric radiators or mobile gas-fired radiators. Underfloor electric heating is not yet common other than in very expensive properties and is very costly to run. Many new properties do come equipped with pre-installation facilities for air-conditioning and heating. The air-conditioning unit in summer becomes a heater in the winter. However, the heat produced by this method is a very dry heat and can't usually be used for long periods. Gas is the cheapest method of heating after logs and although many areas don't yet have mains gas connections, large bottles of propane gas can be an efficient method of heating.

'May I see some recent utility bills to get an idea of how much it will cost to run this property?'

Yes, your lawyer can ask for these bills so that you can get an idea of what the property will cost to run. Running expenses must be taken into consideration before you finally commit yourself to the property because they are non-negotiable and will increase in the future. If you can't afford to pay the electricity or phone bills your service will be cut, it's as simple as that. Providers do not look at your circumstances before they disconnect you or send warning letters as they might in the UK – they simply cut you off.

Local taxes will increase automatically in line with inflation, and urbanisation charges usually increase on an annual basis.

Your lawyer should have checked that all local taxes, utility bills, outstanding mortgages and community charges have been paid to date. You, however, should check what they will cost you in the future and make sure that on your budget you can afford them, not just now but in the longer term. If you're buying a property and are going to live in it all year round, check that your income will be sufficient to pay all the bills and leave you with a realistic amount to live on.

If you plan to let your property and your estate agent tells you that you will be able to let it for 25 weeks a year, then make your financial plans for a rental income based on 10 weeks. Don't plan to use the property yourself in July and August because that is the time when you will get the highest occupation rates and the highest prices.

We know people who have villas in Spain who actually move out of their own home in July and August so that they can capitalise on the rental income they can generate from their home. A bit of an upheaval in the short-term because they have to clear their personal possessions out of their own home, but they consider it worthwhile because it increases their annual income.

 ## 'What will it cost me to build a new house?'

This is a difficult question because it very much depends on what you want to build and where you plan to build it. If you only want to build a basic house with very few modern amenities then you probably need to bargain for around €800 per square metre. So a 150 square metre house could cost €120,000 on top of the cost of the land.

If you want a really good construction with cavity walls and better finishes generally then you should bargain for €1000 per square metre so the same 150 square metre house will potentially cost you €150,000 to build.

If your dream and your budget stretches to a really luxurious property with state-of-the-art fixtures and fittings, expensive tiled floors and walls and landscaped gardens then the sky's the limit. Prices will vary dramatically depending on where you want to build. Labour costs in coastal areas are far higher than those in more rural areas.

On top of the actual building costs there will be other fees which you will have to pay. Architects will generally charge between 5 and 10 per cent of the building costs but this can sometimes be negotiated downwards. You also need to budget for a project manager who will always be on site and can co-ordinate local builders and craftsmen, especially if you're not living in Spain. Your architect should organise the necessary building permits and licences, safety studies, geological reports and any other requirements during the construction process. The architect will usually require around 70 per cent of his fee once building starts and the balance is due on completion when the town hall or the regional government issue the *certificado de fin de obra nueva* (certificate of new work), the *liciencia de primera ocupación* (licence for the first occupation) and the *cédula de habitabilidad* which declares the house is fit to live in. All these various fees can add between 16 and 19 per cent to the cost of building so budget for €20,000 to €30,000 on top of the figures quoted above for a basic and good construction.

Summary

In this chapter I have tried to deal with questions related to the cost of buying and running your house in Spain. These are very important questions because future costs should be considered along with the immediate cost of buying. I have also dealt with the questions of how much it will cost to renovate or build a new house from the ground up.

Glossary

Certificado de fin de obra nueva   certificate of new work

Liciencia de primera ocupación   licence for the first occupation

Cédula de habitabilidad   certificate which declares the house is fit to live in

Impuesto sobre Bienes Inmuebles (IBI)   local tax

Impuesto sobre Actos Jurídicos Documentados (AJD)   Stamp Duty

Impuesto de Transmisiones Patrimoniales (ITP)   transfer tax

Patrimonio   wealth tax

Plus valía   a local property tax levied on the increased value of the land since it was last sold

representante fiscal   tax representative

todos los gastos   literally all the costs. Make sure this is not on the sale document or you will have to pay the vendor's costs as well s your own.

valor catastral   rateable value

Chapter 7

What steps should I take to buy my chosen property?

 'What should I do before I make an offer?'

Find yourself an experienced, English-speaking independent lawyer, called an *abogado*, who will be ready to act on your behalf when you find the right property. If you already know people who live locally they may be able to advise you. Word-of-mouth recommendations are usually the best. Similarly a good estate agent who offers a really personal service will have good contacts, although always be careful that there is no financial interest for them in the recommendation. If you're buying a new property, never use the services of the lawyers acting for the developers because they can't possibly be independent.

They are primarily acting for the vendor. This is also the stage when your lawyer may suggest you use the services of a *gestor*, potentially your best friend in Spain. His role is explained below.

There is one formal piece of paperwork which you must obtain before you buy a holiday home or relocate permanently to Spain, and that is to register yourself for what is known as a *NIE* number. Its full title is *Número de Identificación de* Extranjero (Foreigner's Identification Number). This is your tax identification number which will help the Spanish tax authorities to identify you. You can't undertake any major financial or official transactions in Spain without one. You can't legally complete the purchase of your chosen property, you can't open a bank account, or apply for a Spanish mortgage, you can't sign up to pay your utility bills, organise house, car, health or life insurance without one and you will find it difficult to buy a car without the magic *NIE* number.

The process of obtaining an *NIE* number is actually very straightforward but can take several weeks, so it's important that you apply as early as possible. You can't apply until you have made an offer on a property since you need to be able to put a Spanish address on the application form. If you are renting you can apply with your rental address or if you have made an offer for a business you can use that address. What you cannot do is to apply for an *NIE* number simply as a tourist who might be interested in buying property in Spain

You need to visit your nearest national police station which may have a counter for foreigners, or an interpreter, if it's an area popular with expats. You will also need to take along your passport, a photocopy of your passport and several passport-size photographs. Fill in the appropriate form and your *NIE* number will usually be issued in a few weeks. The delay varies depending on the area and the time of year.

If you are not there in person, your *gestor* can obtain your *NIE* on your behalf as long as he has the relevant paperwork. If you understand a little Spanish you should be able to complete the form or your *gestor* can help you with that too. A good *gestor* may be able to speed up the process for you because they have good contacts and they always know the right people to speak to.

Once you have your *NIE* number you can open a Spanish bank account. This will make it much easier to transfer money from your home country to Spain when you come to complete the purchase. It will also make it far easier if you want to raise a Spanish mortgage. If you don't have a Spanish bank account, any money which you transfer will have to be paid into a bonded account either with your lawyer or with the estate agent.

'What exactly is a gestor?'

Quite simply the best friend you might ever have in Spain. A *gestor* is not a lawyer or financial adviser but usually works alongside them and is an intermediary between you and Spanish bureaucracy. When you're trying to get things done in Spain, it really does matter who you know and a good *gestor* knows everyone who matters. The *gestor* knows how council and local government offices work and will often achieve the results you want far quicker than you could do yourself even if you speak fluent Spanish. I looked up the term in my Spanish dictionary and it did not exist because there is no UK equivalent. It's a licensed profession that solely exists to help both Spaniards and foreigners complete the necessary paperwork correctly, submit it to the right authorities on time and ring the right people when they are needed.

In Spain, as in many countries, local bureaucracy can be very slow and everything has to be followed absolutely to the letter. The *gestor* knows and understands these procedures and will guide you through this potential bureaucratic nightmare. What's more, his fees are extremely reasonable. Spaniards also use the services of a *gestor* because they know that they are appointing the services of someone who really knows and understands the system which even many Spaniards don't understand.

In a Spanish town of any size you will find several *gestores* listed in the telephone directory. If you have a good estate agent, they should be able to direct you to a good local *gestor*. If the question draws a blank on the agent's face, find another agent because the person you are talking to knows very little about Spain!

If your first purchase in Spain is intended initially as a holiday home, a *gestor* is even more important. He will be able to ensure that all your utility bills are paid on time, even when you are not there and that your holiday home will be there and waiting for you with no problems whenever you go back.

'What can a gestor do for you if you're either a permanent resident or a non-resident with property?'

gestores can carry out all administrative procedures and look after your income tax and wealth tax if necessary. Remember in Spain if you buy and are officially a non-resident you will receive a notional income tax demand every year because the Spanish government assumes that you are renting the property. This bill can be sent to your *gestor* who will deal with it on your behalf. A *gestor* can also look after your local taxes (*IBI*) and your car tax for any vehicles registered in Spain.

A *gestor* can also help you with the paperwork involved in importing a vehicle into Spain (although there are huge numbers of British registered vehicles which have never been officially imported!) and he can help you to obtain a Spanish driving licence. When you want to sell a vehicle, he can also help you with the transfer of the official documents to a new owner. Selling a vehicle in Spain is much more complicated than doing the same thing in the UK.

If you need insurance for your house, your car, your health or for your life, your *gestor* is often also an insurance agent.

If you want to set up a business in Spain your *gestor*, alongside an *asesoria fiscal* (specialist financial adviser) can also help you with this and provide advice.

Once you are established in Spain, your *gestor*, alongside an experienced lawyer, can give you advice on preparing a Spanish will and also liaise with the local notary to make sure that the will is properly signed and registered.

As I said above, the *gestor* can be your best friend in Spain and their services are not expensive. Using a *gestor* could be one of the best investments you ever make during your time in Spain.

 ### 'How do I make an offer?'

This is no different from making an offer in any other country. You have seen a property you like, you want to buy, and you can discuss with the agent whether or not the seller is likely to accept a reasonable offer below the asking price. When prices are rising fast, the vendor may not be prepared to negotiate but if the market is slow, buyers can be lucky and get a good price. This is why you should keep a careful eye on the way the market is moving in your chosen area.

The same applies if you are a vendor. If the market is slow it might be better to accept a reasonable offer for a quick sale rather than hold out for the asking price which you might never achieve in the short term. When we sold our last apartment we accepted an offer almost 20 per cent lower than the value placed on it by several local estate agents but we sold and relatively quickly. If we had held out for the asking price we might still be trying to sell. Properties in that particular area are moving very slowly unless the price is right. Some have been on the market for two years or more. Don't buy at the asking price unless the property is truly unique and could never be matched. If your lawyer agrees and it's appropriate for your situation, you also need to agree about whether part of the price will be in cash, for fixtures and fittings. Increasingly lawyers are advising against this and telling their clients that the price on the *escritura* should include everything.

You will also notice that, particularly in coastal areas, property is often sold furnished. If the property has been used as a holiday home it can be cheaper for the vendor to leave all the furniture, and fixtures and fittings behind rather than organise their removal. If the furnishings are good quality, you may be able to buy a very nice home, ready to move into, but you should ask for an inventory of what is to be left. Your estate agent, particularly if they are local can usually organise this for you.

Just before completion someone, either yourself, the agent or your lawyer, should visit the property to check that everything on the inventory is still there. There have been occasions when the buyer has paid for a furnished property only to find that all the good quality furniture they originally saw has been removed and replaced with that of an inferior quality.

'What are the legal implications in making an offer?'

There are no legal implications in making an offer, but once the offer has been accepted and you pay a deposit into a bonded bank account, held by the agent or by your lawyer, then you're committed. Until this happens you can withdraw the offer, increase the offer or continue looking at other properties. In the same way, even if your offer is accepted the vendor is not legally obliged to take the property off the market until you have paid a deposit. Once the deposit has been paid, it's unlikely that the vendor will change their mind because if they do they must return twice the amount of your deposit. This makes gazumping very unusual.

 ## 'What happens next?'

If your offer is accepted the agent will confirm this and then you have to contact your lawyer to set the process in motion. If you haven't already started this process, this is when you should register for an *NIE* number.

'What deposit will I have to pay?'

The first step you will be asked to take is to sign a *contrato privado de compraventa* (a private contract between yourself and the vendor). This is not a legal requirement and you can go straight to the notary and ask him to draw up the deed, but if you're paying a deposit, which you normally do at this stage, you must have a contract. When this contract is signed a non-refundable deposit is paid, usually 10 per cent of the purchase price. This deposit must be held in a special bonded bank account held by the vendor's lawyer or the estate agent and the receipt should state that if there are any problems with the property, the money will be returned to you. It's vital that the money is held in a bonded bank account and only released when you sign the appropriate documents. Then you are protected if you find yourself dealing with individuals whose scruples are not what they should be. The last thing you need at this stage is to find that your money has disappeared.

When you pay the deposit, you should sign what is known as a *contrato de arras* (a deposit contract) and there are two different types, depending on your circumstances. The first is called the *arras de desistimiento* and this allows the buyer to pull out of the sale, although they would lose their deposit. If the vendor pulls out, they would have to pay the potential buyer twice the amount of the deposit. The second type of deposit is called the *arras confirmatoria* and this can't be cancelled by either party. This is less common and should only be used if your lawyer recommends it. Make sure you know the conditions of your deposit before you sign anything. When the deposit has been paid you are well on the way to owning your property in Spain.

You should make sure that your lawyer inserts any necessary conditional clauses in the contract and checks those that the vendor has requested. Conditional clauses can include almost anything that the buyer and vendor agree to, but they are usually conditions such as the buyer being able to raise a mortgage, obtain planning permission or subject to a satisfactory survey on the property. Then if any of these things don't go according to plan, the contract can be cancelled without any penalties. If you don't have these clauses put in and a problem arises then you could lose your deposit and may even be forced to go ahead with the sale.

The property must also be as described on the *escritura publica* or the *nota simple* (short form of the *escritura*). If it's not, you can withdraw from the sale without penalty and have your deposit returned. The first property we made an offer on was a new build and we had paid a small holding deposit. It was a ground floor apartment and was described as having a private garden. When we went to our lawyer's office to pay the official deposit we discovered that the private garden did not officially exist because it was classified as common land. We were also going to be asked to pay the *plus valía* tax (see the previous chapter) which is normally paid by the vendor or developer on the increased value of land. As we were cash buyers, we were also going to be charged for the loss of commission which the developer would have received if he had organised our mortgage. We did not want a mortgage so why should we pay for the loss of commission to the developer? We felt that we had been misled and our lawyer actually managed to get our deposit refunded. If we had decided to use the services of the lawyer acting for the developer, it's unlikely that our deposit would ever have been refunded.

'What can I usefully do before signing the initial contract?'

Before committing yourself totally to a purchase it could be useful to return to the property, without the agent, so that you can try to meet some of your potential future neighbours and find out what it's really like to live there. It's always good to make sure that you're not letting your heart rule your head. If you decide that this really is where you want to be, this is the time to organise such mundane things as bank accounts and making sure your finance for the purchase is in place.

'How do I open a bank account?'

It's usually best to wait until you know exactly where you want to live before you open a bank account. The nearest branch of your chosen bank should be close to your home unless you want to do all your banking via the Internet or use telephone banking. So once you have chosen your property, you should visit the bank.

Opening a bank account is very easy, particularly if you either have a good local estate agent who can recommend a bank and introduce you personally to the manager. Alternatively, if you have friends who live in the same area, ask them for their opinions of the bank and if they can introduce you to the manager. Otherwise you can simply present yourself to one of the local banks and say that you would like to open an account.

In the coastal areas you will find that the majority of banks have English-speaking staff which can make things easier and they are all hungry for your business. Many of them will provide you with a regular statement in English, which is far easier than trying to decipher the Spanish statement using your Spanish dictionary.

Another option is to open an account in Spain with the Spanish branch of the bank you already use in your own country. This is usually easy to do and one major benefit of using the same bank in both countries is that commission charges are often waived or reduced on transfers between accounts in the two countries. This can be a big bonus. You could open this type of account before you decide finally on your chosen property, but you might find that your 'local' branch is a long way from where you live. As a result all your banking will need to be done by telephone or Internet. For many people, this is not a big problem; it just depends on your personal preference.

Spanish banking is generally very good and all the services you would expect are available, such as counter service, loans and mortgages, telephone and Internet banking. However, Spanish bank charges are amongst the highest in Europe, even for the most routine services. If you don't need a monthly statement, don't have one because you will be charged for each one. We also found that each time a standing order or a direct debit was made from our account we received a letter from the bank to confirm the transaction, but we had to pay for each letter. The bank is simply looking for any way they can to make money from the customer, so make sure you inform them, in writing, of your requirements.

There can also be delays in the transfer of money to your Spanish bank from banks in other countries and this could cause you serious problems. If the *notario* does not have your money in his account on the day you complete on the sale, it will not go ahead. If the money you are transferring to pay your utility bills is not in your account on the day they are due, the bills will not be paid. You really need to transfer funds using one of the new systems of money transfer such as via the International Bank Account Number (IBAN) system or the electronic SWIFT system. It costs a little bit more but is quicker and worth it to have the money available when you need it.

For any readers who are retired there is one more important point; if your UK state pension is paid directly into your Spanish bank account in euros there should be no commission charged. Charging is contrary to EU law but many charge transfer fees as well as a further fee just to receive the money. If you discover that commission is being charged, often a simple letter to your bank will result in any charge being waived and previous charges refunded.

Q 'What happens if I have not yet raised the necessary money to fund the purchase?'

You don't need to have all the necessary funds in place to make an offer. Even if you don't have a bank account in Spain the deposit can be transferred from any account, such as your UK bank account, to the bonded account of the estate agent or lawyer. Until the deposit has been paid the vendor can continue to show the property and accept another offer. Neither party has any contractual obligations until the deposit has been paid.

Many estate agents operating in Spain often have very good links with mortgage brokers and can help you to raise the finance to buy your dream property.

Finance is usually available to buy a Spanish property even if you don't have the actual cash in your pocket. However, in the current economic climate (2008), banks are operating stricter loan conditions because of global financial concerns and a universal credit crunch by lenders. Up until fairly recently it was a very different story in Spain. We know of people who have visited one mortgage broker to ask for a 50 per cent mortgage which was approved. The next step was to visit a second mortgage broker to ask for a 50 per cent mortgage which was also approved. As a result a 100 per cent mortgage was possible. This may sound like good news but if a broker arranges a mortgage for you, make sure you know what the repayment terms are. Sometimes brokers might arrange a mortgage where the repayments are initially low but may increase over time. The brokers are sailing close to the wind to earn commission on setting up any mortgage they can - they are not usually interested in the client's needs, so make sure you get the product that suits your needs.

When we sold one of our properties our buyer was able to obtain a 110 per cent mortgage on the asking price because he wanted to redecorate the apartment. This was good for us because we wanted to sell, but it was rather irresponsible of him and his lender because property prices can also fall, a trend which we are already beginning to see. For this buyer, that kind of borrowing can result in negative equity.

Q 'Will I be able to obtain a UK mortgage for a Spanish property?'

The best way to buy property in Spain is to use the capital on your UK property and buy in cash. UK lenders can't directly give you a mortgage on a Spanish property because they can't secure a charge on it. However, it you have equity in your UK home you can borrow money secured on that equity, rather than take out a Spanish mortgage.

If you do need a mortgage, your first stop should be either your UK bank or a Spanish bank. Avoid mortgage brokers unless you are really desperate to raise the money. The chances are that if you have any problems in the future the broker will no longer be in business.

If you decide to apply for a UK based loan, the repayments will be in sterling and therefore not subject to prevailing exchange rates, as long as your income is and remains in sterling. As a result you will know exactly what your repayments will be over the loan period. If you take out a mortgage in Spain the repayments will be in euros and could be affected by changes in the value of the euro. This will not matter if your income is in euros, but will make a difference if it's in sterling.

For example, when we first moved to Spain in 2001, had we had monthly mortgage payments of €160 this would have been equivalent to £100. Today that monthly payment would be equivalent to £120. Although this is not a big difference, it could be another story if you have a bigger mortgage. Exchange rate fluctuations can have a big effect on your monthly repayments.

Q 'How can I obtain a loan in Spain to buy the property?'

Simply apply to the Spanish bank where you have an account. You may find their terms are less flexible than those in your home country, and some lenders are stricter about income and the type of property on which they will lend. Remember too that this mortgage will be in euros and the repayments will be in euros so the costs will vary depending on the exchange rate.

Q 'Should I get a survey carried out?'

A full structural survey is not a normal practice in the purchase of Spanish property and Spanish mortgages are not normally granted subject to survey. If a buyer is worried about the state of the property they often ask a local builder they know or someone has been recommended to them to have a look at the house and say what they think about it. If the builder is a friend this will probably cost nothing. If you bring a surveyor from the

UK to look at a property you might never buy it. This is because the surveyor will naturally look at your proposed purchase and apply UK standards to it. He will probably report that there is no damp-proof course, the electrics are not on a ring main, etc. etc. Unless your UK surveyor understands Spanish building practices, the report will be horrifying. Spanish surveyors do exist and if you would prefer to have a survey done, ask your estate agent or lawyer for reliable recommendations.

'What documentation should the seller provide before completion of the sale?'

One of the first things your lawyer will do is obtain proof that the seller is the legal owner of the property and has the right to sell it. They should also obtain written confirmation that the property is free of all debts; mortgages, utility bills, unpaid taxes and maintenance charges. If there are any problems with these documents, it could be the first sign that something is wrong. The vendor should provide a copy of the *escritura* (title deeds) and your lawyer will initially obtain a *referencia catastral* (registration number of the property) and the *nota simple* (an extract of the *escritura*) from the *Registro de la Propiedad* (Spanish Property Register). This will prove that the vendor actually owns the property and is entitled to sell it. It will also tell you the size of the property and if there are any charges, such as a mortgage or any court embargoes, against it. Remember if you buy a property which has an outstanding mortgage you will be responsible for any remaining payments.

The *nota simple* confirms exactly who owns the property, all of whom will have to sign the final documents on the day of the completion of the sale. There have been occasions when one of the owners has actually died but the death was not communicated to the Spanish authorities as the owners did not live there permanently. As a result, on the day of completion a legal signatory was missing so completion had to be aborted. The same thing could happen if an old property has been left to a family. Every inheritor will need to sign the documents on completion of the sale. This is often a reason why an old country property can't be sold - because one or more family members can't be traced.

Your lawyer will also need to see copies of the most recent receipts for local taxes (*IBI*) and any other utility bills to prove that these have been paid. If they have not been paid you will inherit the charges.

Q 'How can I make sure the property matches the vendor's or agent's description?'

Your lawyer will use the *Referencia Catastral* (property registration number) to obtain a *nota simple*. The *Referencia Catastral* appears on the receipt for local taxes (*IBI*). The *Certificado Catastral* (Cadastral Certificate) will describe the property with respect to floor area, the number of rooms and if it has land, the area of the land. The document should also include a plan or an aerial photograph of the land which belongs to the property. If the description of your proposed purchase does not match the description exactly you or your lawyer need to ask questions. If you're buying an apartment you should check the floor area against that on the description provided by the agent or the owner. Often the real floor area will be less and this could be used as a bargaining tool. Look out for extra rooms; if you think you're buying a five-bedroom house but the official documents say it is a three-bedroom house then alarm bells should ring. The additional two bedrooms may be illegal and have no planning permission.

If you're doubtful about the real area of any land which you are buying in the country you can arrange for an official land surveyor to come and measure the area of the land. Your lawyer should be able to recommend one. Always check any verbal description often made by the estate agent that 'the land extends up to the trees you can see on the top of the hill over there'. This is a recipe for long-term arguments over your boundaries. Ideally the land should be delineated by some sort of boundary fence. On the day of completion of the sale the *notario* might actually notice that there are discrepancies and ask you to sign a document to say that you were aware of this. Once you sign this document you will have no legal comeback.

If you're buying in an area which is already classified as urban land or is in the process of being urbanised, you should also ask your lawyer to look at proposed plans for new roads, railways or other planned developments in your area. The last thing you want is a new motorway or railway line at the end of your garden.

'If I am buying in an urbanisation what extra steps should be taken?'

Your lawyer will find out a lot by referring to the *plan parcial* for the area if you are buying in an urbanisation. As described earlier this plan is held by the local authority and will tell you if planning permission and building permits are in order and whether the urbanisation was built according to the plan. It should show the long-term plan for the area and how this will affect the various *parcelas* (plots) of land in the urbanisation. Some will be designated for apartments, some for townhouses or villas, some as green space and some for commercial development. All of these proposed developments will need access roads.

If you are buying in an urbanisation, the vendor should also provide you with proof that all annual community fees for the upkeep of common areas have been paid. It's now a legal requirement for the vendor to produce a certificate from the community to confirm that payments are up to date. These must be presented to the *notario* on completion.

If you're buying an apartment, a townhouse or a villa in an urbanisation you should also ask your lawyer to obtain a copy of the rules of the urbanisation. Your lawyer should check these rules and your obligations very carefully. When you sign the final documents you will be bound by these rules and if they state, for example, that no pets are allowed in the property, you could have problems if the President of the urbanisation strictly adheres to these rules. On the other hand after you have moved in and you have developed a good relationship with the President, you might find that the rules might be relaxed for you. Our urbanisation banned pets but we had two dogs. We had a good relationship with the President so we had no problems.

You can also ask to see the minutes of previous AGMs of the management committee of the urbanisation. It is amazing how many potential problems can be unearthed by reading these minutes. There might have been ongoing problems with plumbing, sewage, painting, garden or swimming pool maintenance, non-payment of fees and many other factors. Any one of these could set alarm bells ringing and affect your decision to buy.

Q 'How can I check that the property fulfils all legal requirements?'

Your lawyer should ask to see the documents which show that your property has been built legally. If it is a new property you should ask for the proof that the property has a *certificado de fin de obra nueva* (certificate of new work) to state that it has been completed, and approved by the local authority in accordance with the building plans. It should also have a *licencia de primera ocupación* (licence for first occupation). If you don't have these you can't be connected to any utilities. If the appropriate certificates have not been issued by the Town Hall your wonderful new property could actually be illegally constructed and therefore unable to be registered – it could even face a demolition order.

We know of people who were unable to sign up for electricity, water or a telephone service because officially their new property did not yet exist. The developers simply told them not to worry and to just go on using the developer's electricity, water and their own mobile phone until the property was officially approved! They thought this was wonderful because they would have no bills until this happened. You need to be very careful indeed about doing this kind of thing. Even the developer's electricity supply could be illegal. We discovered that the developers in our urbanisation had tapped into the street lighting cables to supply them with electricity for building purposes. This was one occasion when a *denuncia* produced a very rapid result!

If you're buying new property close to the sea you also need to ask your lawyer to check that the construction is totally legal. As I described earlier sea views do command higher prices and many new properties have been built right on the beach. However a law introduced in 1988, the *Ley de Costas* (coastal law) restricted new building above a certain height or density built within 105 metres of the high water mark. Many older properties built before 1988 right on the beach will be legal but some new ones could be illegal. Developers have been known to build sea barriers which push the high water mark further out to sea.

Just as I was completing this book I picked up information that the central Government in Madrid has announced proposals which are now law and which could lead to the demolition of many of these properties which have been built illegally since 1988. Indeed one unlucky British couple have already had their home demolished recently in Almeria.

Spain is starting to take note of how the coastal area is being destroyed by over-development. According to the new documents, 30 per cent of the Spanish Mediterranean coast, 51 per cent of the beaches and 70 per cent of the dune areas are now enclosed by building and development. Anyone considering the purchase of a property right on the beachfront needs to be aware of the potential problems and make sure their property does not contravene the *Ley de Costas*.

If you're buying a plot of land, whether near to the coast or in the countryside on which you plan to build a property, you should ask for absolute written confirmation that building permission for the kind of property you want has been granted. This is why there are so many 'illegal' properties. The land was bought and someone simply built a house on it without applying for planning permission. In addition, many buyers have obtained the correct planning permission but unfortunately that permission was granted by corrupt council officials. The buyers are the innocent party but often the authorities don't see it that way. Your lawyer must check with the Town Hall that the land is classified as urban land and may be built on and is not classified totally as *rústico*, rural land.

Summary

In this chapter I have tried to deal with all the points about making an offer on a property, appointing someone who can act as an adviser, the legal implications of making an offer, deposits, contracts, opening bank accounts in Spain, funding and mortgages, surveys, documentation and possible problem areas to watch out for.

Glossary

abogado	lawyer
gestor	an expert in Spanish bureaucracy
Número de Identificación de Extranjero	Foreigner's Identification Number.
contrato privado de compraventa	private contract between vendor and buyer
arras de desistiamento	a refundable deposit if all conditions are not met
arras confirmatoria deposit	a totally non-refundable
Escritura Pública	title deeds (official copy held in Property Registry)
Ley de Costas	coastal Law relating to building on the beach front
nota simple	a short form of the *escritura*

Chapter 8

What are the stages of the contractual process?

When your offer is accepted, your lawyer should check and double-check all the relevant documents before you pay any deposit and sign the appropriate forms.

 'What is the initial stage of the contractual process?'

Once your lawyer has made all the checks discussed in Chapter 6, you will be ready to sign the initial private contract and pay the deposit into a bonded bank account. Before you do this, you should have the contract translated so that you understand what you're signing.

'What are my rights as a buyer at this point?'

Once you have paid your deposit you are committed to the sale unless any of the conditional clauses which you have asked to be included are not met. Chapter 6 has details about conditional clauses. You will lose your deposit if you pull out for any other reason. The vendors forfeit twice the deposit if they decide to pull out without a reason.

 ## 'What is the notary's role in the buying process?'

The *notario* is not a lawyer, he is a representative of the State and his job is to ensure that any transactions, not just property sales, proceed according to the laws of Spain and that everyone is aware of their tax obligations. If you can't be present at this 'ceremony' you can appoint someone with power of attorney on your behalf, called a *poder* in Spain. Your lawyer can arrange this for you or it can be done through the notary's office at a small charge. Your estate agent will often agree to be your *poder* but make sure that you really trust him with this role.

The *notario* must certify that the transaction has taken place according to the property transfer laws and that provision has been made for all appropriate taxes - for example, if you buy from a non-resident in Spain, 3 per cent of their selling price of the property will be retained and paid to the *Agencia Tributaria* or *Hacienda* (tax office) against possible unpaid income tax or Capital Gains Tax. This is one more reason why you should use the services of a lawyer if you are buying a resale property. He will ensure that this percentage is deducted from the proceeds using the appropriate forms and is held by the *notario* for the taxman. The converse also applies; if you sell a property for €200,000 and you can't prove that you are an official tax resident, the *notario* will withhold €6,000 against unpaid taxes.

The *notario* must also certify that the money (the officially agreed amount as declared on the *escritura*) has been transferred. It's not his role to certify that all the documentation has been checked and accepted by the parties in the sales process – this is your lawyer's responsibility.

'What happens in the final stage of the process?'

After all the documentation has been collected, checked and double-checked to your satisfaction the day of completion will arrive when everyone concerned meets in the notary's office to sign the new *Escritura Pública*. The *notario* will check that all conditions in the contract have been fulfilled. The deed is read (in Spanish), signed and witnessed by the *notario*. The deed must be signed by you and any other associated buyers and by all the vendors in the presence of the notary which makes the sale legally binding. At this stage the finance for the sale must be in place either through a personal cheque (if you are a cash buyer either from your Spanish bank or as an international bank draft) or through a proven mortgage document which the mortgage provider will often bring to this meeting. The *notario* keeps a copy of this document in his file to prove that all the correct legal steps have been taken. Once you have paid the money and received a receipt, the *notario* will give you a *copia simple* (an unsigned copy of the deed) which proves that you're the new owner of the property - and the keys!

The signed deed is then forwarded to the *Registro de la Propiedad* (Land Registry) and becomes the *Escritura Pública*. The *notario* should do this within 30 days. One way to speed up the process is to insist that a copy of the signed *escritura* is faxed to the Land Registry on the day you sign it. Many *notarios* do this anyway and it ensures that no-one else can register the property. Registering the new ownership is vitally important because until it's officially registered in your name, you're not the legal owner and charges and mortgages can be registered against it and you will never know. After registration, the deed will be returned to you, via the *notario* or your lawyer. The copy of the *Escritura Pública* should arrive within two to three months of your visit to the *notario*. If it does not arrive you or your lawyer must follow it up with the authorities.

The potential dangers of any delay is that your property could have been in the hands of several estate agents and could have been sold by a vendor who might have been unscrupulous enough to 'sell' to more than one person at the same time. Someone else could actually have made an offer and gone through exactly the same process which you have just followed. The first person to receive the confirmation from the Land Registry will be the legal owner. If this person uses a different notary, this situation might not be noticed for some time. You might have already transferred the purchase price to the vendor who has now conveniently disappeared with your money and has also received the same amount of money from the other buyer who registered the sale before you. Although this is relatively rare, believe me, it can happen, so you must ensure ownership of the property is legally registered in your name as soon as possible.

'How long will the buying process take from start to finish?'

If the process is simple and you're in a rush to buy it could take just a few weeks or, if you have the cash, just a few days, but nothing in life is ever simple so assume that it will take between two and three months from the time that your offer is accepted until the moment that you take possession of the keys to your new property. I would not recommend trying to speed up the process unless you really have to. Cutting corners for a quick purchase could lead to real problems in the future. You're making a very important decision, particularly if you plan to relocate, so it could be a very foolish move to rush into decisions or try to cut corners to speed up the process.

In fact if you do have the cash and your offer is accepted, in theory you could go straight to the notary, hand over the cash and he will prepare the *escritura*. The entire process could actually be completed in a few days. In the past, this was fairly common especially if buyers were trying to 'launder' money. After all, putting what's known as black money into a property which the buyer then sells on very quickly is a sneaky way of legitimising that money. These days, however, that is far harder to do because the authorities have brought in tough new laws to prevent money-laundering through property purchases. The sources of any money used to pay for a property must be accounted for. Recently, there have been several highly-publicised arrests of officials, including lawyers and notaries, particularly in coastal areas of Spain and so you will find that they are unwilling to be associated with any kind of transaction that may be deemed suspicious.

Q 'What should I do about the inheritance tax laws at this point?'

You need to consider the *Impuesto sobre sucesiones* (Inheritance tax) at this stage. Spanish law does not always offer a large exemption from inheritance tax even between official partners who are classified as a non-resident. Your property will not automatically be inherited by your partner on your death so make sure that you discuss your personal situation with your lawyer. Exemptions depend on the beneficiary's relationship with the deceased and whether you are a resident or non-resident. Tax is calculated on a sliding scale ranging from just under 8 per cent to 34 per cent, depending on your circumstances.

If you're classified as a resident and you leave the property to your partner or to your children you may be eligible for up to 99 per cent reduction in the tax base. However, the property must be your principal residence and you must have been officially resident in the property for at least three years. In addition, the inheritors must also be resident and undertake not to sell it for 10 years. However even this exemption has a sting in the tail since it only applies to estates worth up to €120,000. Non-residents cannot take advantage of this exemption so a holiday home could attract a lot of inheritance tax.

There are two ways around what appear to be quite draconian inheritance tax laws and these are to buy the property either through a family trust or through an offshore company. With the former the family's wealth passes to the trust and each member of the family becomes a director of the trust. If one of the directors should die it only needs a re-arrangement of the board of directors (at a small cost) and a transfer of shares between the trust members. The latter requires you to set up a company outside Spain which buys the property and if you die you leave your shares to whoever you like. Because a company does not 'die' there is no inheritance tax but you will have to pay Spanish income tax every year on the company. Spanish inheritance tax is a very complicated subject and you really need to discuss these topics with a lawyer as well as a financial adviser.

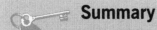 # Summary

The property purchase procedure differs from country to country and before you take any major steps you should understand these differences. Buying in Spain is not difficult if you know the rules.

- **What is the buying process in Spain?**
- **How do I make an offer on property?**
- **What deposit will I have to make?**
- **How long will the buying process take?**
- **What other formalities should I know about?**
- **When and how should I open a bank account in Spain?**
- **What should I do about inheritance tax?**

A checklist for anyone buying a property in Spain:

- **Appoint your own independent Spanish lawyer who is acting only for you.**
- **Obtain a copy of the *nota simple* and the vendor's *Escritura Pública*.**
- **Obtain details of the *Certificado Catastral*.**
- **Check on the legal status of the property, the *plan parcial* if you are buying in an urbanisation or a copy of the planning permission if you are buying a plot of land on which you plan to build.**
- **Confirmation in writing that all taxes, community charges and utility bills have been paid up to the date of sale.**
- **Documents which you fully understand if you are going to sign them. This may mean paying for a translation.**
- **Confirmation from the notary as to when you will receive the final *Escritura Pública* which will confirm your ownership of the property.**

Glossary

Agencia Tributaria or Hacienda	the tax office
copia simple	an unsigned copy of the deeds
Certificado Catastral	certificate from the cadastral office showing boundaries, internal and external details of the property.
poder	power of attorney
Impuesto sobre sucesiones	Inheritance tax

Chapter 9

What happens after I've bought the property?

Once you have completed the sale, you, your family, your friendly estate agent and anyone else important to you will probably want to visit the nearest bar and order a bottle of *cava* (Spanish champagne/sparkling wine) to celebrate the fact that you now own your dream property in Spain. However, to establish yourself in your new property and begin your new life in Spain there are certain things which you will have to address in the short-, medium- and long-term.

 'What checks should I carry out on the property?'

Now that you have the keys you should take the opportunity to visit your new home and check that all the windows can be locked securely and that the shutters close securely. You can also check where the master switch is to turn off the electricity and where the stopcock is to turn off the water. No-one ever shows you these things during the viewing process but they are vital to the long term security of the property. The next thing you should do is to change the locks. If the property has been unoccupied during the sales process, it could have been in the hands of several estate agents and each one could have had a key in order to arrange viewings.

'How do I go about changing over the utilities?'

This is one area where we have never had a problem. Each time we have moved the change over from the previous owner has been absolutely simple. However, we have always left the arrangements in the hands of our friendly local estate agent, who is a fluent Spanish speaker. You can do this yourself but it's far easier if someone who knows and understands the system does it for you and it should be part of the estate agent's service.

You might think that I am putting a lot of emphasis on the estate agent but for 5 per cent commission, I believe you should take advantage of all the services they offer.

'How can I arrange the change over of electricity supply?'

When you know the completion date, your lawyer should arrange that the meter is read on that day and that your electricity supplier is informed of a change of owner. Your lawyer must insist on the meter being read on the day of completion and can probably also organise the transfer. If not, your estate agent can probably help with this. During the last few years, the utilities market in Spain has been liberalised, but you still get little choice about who provides you electricity. There will be one company who supplies to your region.

If you buy in a more rural part of Spain you should have checked long before now that electricity can be supplied to your property and if not, have made alternative power arrangements.

'How can I arrange the change over of gas or oil supply?'

This is fairly easy to deal with because apart from a few big cities, Spain does not have mains gas. The majority of consumers use gas which is supplied in bottles. On every occasion we have bought in Spain we have inherited one or more gas bottles and it is very simple to take the empty bottle back to the local garage, supermarket, etc. and exchange it for a full bottle. Should the previous owner be so mean as to take the old bottles, or if you require the large bottles of propane, then all you have to do is to go to the nearest gas distributor, sign a deposit contract and either take home a bottle of gas or they will deliver for you. If you inherit oil-fired central heating your estate agent or lawyer should be able to put you in touch with a supplier.

'How can I arrange the change over of water supply?'

In urbanisations the cost of water supply is normally included in the community charges so there is nothing you have to do when you move in. If you buy an independent property your lawyer or estate agent can arrange for the water bills to be changed into your name. If you buy in a remote country area you might find that you will be dependent on well water.

'How can I arrange the change over of the telephone?'

If your property is a resale then it probably already has a telephone line. In remote country areas a mainline telephone service could still be very difficult. We have friends who have to depend on mobiles or a satellite telephone service. Once more the lawyer or the agent can arrange for this to be transferred into your name from midday on the day of completion. The old number will be cancelled and you will be informed of a new number from *Telefónica*, the main telephone provider in Spain. They have a very good English language helpline. *Telefónica* must provide the actual line but once established with them you are then free to sign up with one of the many services which offer reduced price telephone calls. Many of them advertise in the English-language newspapers available on the coast. We use Spantel which is very good and reasonably priced but there are many others.

If you need a broadband connection, perhaps for business purposes, you can have this connected at the same time. However, you should check before you finalise any sale that it's possible to have a broadband connection in your area. This could affect whether or not you decide to make an offer on the property, especially if your business depends on good Internet service.

Note that the electricity and telephone suppliers are very quick to cut off the service if you do not pay on time - often within two weeks – unlike the UK they don't send a warning letter. Therefore in the early days of your new Spanish adventure if you're not there every day to receive the bills you really should arrange for them to be paid by direct debit. Do not depend on the bills being sent to a UK address so that you can send a cheque from the UK. The Spanish postal system is notoriously slow and could cause you problems.

I fell foul of this not with utility bills but with a major credit card company. Since their billing office was in the Far East, my monthly statement was sent from there via Amsterdam and the UK to Spain. Therefore the date on the bill was almost always three weeks earlier than the date it arrived in Spain. Even if I paid that day it was taking up to three weeks for the payment to be credited to my account so I built up a record of late payments and the card was cancelled. If you continue to use your UK credit cards, I would strongly suggest that you set up a direct debit arrangement so that at least the minimum payment is made each month.

'How can I make sure services don't get cut off in my absence?'

Pay everything by direct debit and do not depend on the postal service which is notoriously slow in Spain. If you still live in the UK it could take one to two weeks for bills to reach you and the same time for your cheque to arrive back in Spain. Often the service providers only give you two weeks to pay the bill before they disconnect and if this happens you will then need to visit their nearest office to pay the bill and possibly also a reconnection charge. If you pay by direct debit, you will still receive the bills and you can check them and if they appear to be inaccurate challenge them, but at least you will not have the inconvenience of being cut off.

'How do I insure the property and contents?'

You need to organise house and contents insurance, either through an insurance agent already known to you, or via the estate agent who handled the sale or with your *gestor*. From my experience this is relatively inexpensive in Spain when compared with prices in the UK. However, there is probably not a huge difference if you buy in one of the large Spanish cities or the very busy holiday areas such as Benidorm or Marbella where there is more crime. You also need to check what the insurance will cover. If you have bought an apartment in an urbanisation the chances are that you only need contents insurance since the fabric of the building will be covered by a common policy as part of the community charge. This may also apply to townhouses but probably not to individual villas in an urbanisation. Independent villas, village townhouses and country properties will require separate cover for the fabric of the building plus the contents.

'How do I organise medical insurance?'

If your property is to be used as a holiday home and your main base remains in the UK then you need to ensure that you have a European Health Insurance Card (EHIC) – this was previously known as an E111 - for each member of the family. This is available from your local UK post office or online at https://www.ehic.org.uk. The EHIC will provide emergency cover while you are travelling in the European Union (EU) but must not be used if you're living abroad permanently. If you do use it this way, it could be considered fraudulent use and you may be asked to refund the full cost of your treatment.

The best thing to do is get hold of the leaflet provided by the Department for Work and Pensions (DWP). This leaflet, SA29 covers your social security insurance, benefits and healthcare rights within the European Economic Area and can be downloaded from the Internet, or if you do not have

Internet access the DWP will send you a copy and it should also be available at larger Post Offices in the UK.

If you're going to live in Spain permanently, you need to obtain an E106 form from the Department for Work and Pensions ideally before you leave Britain. Assuming that you have made National Insurance contributions almost to the date of departure, this form will provide for any medical treatment you may have in Spain to be charged back to the NHS for up to two years. After that, if you're below retirement age, you must either contribute to the Spanish social security system or take out a private healthcare policy. Your *gestor* should be able to recommend a suitable private insurance company, or you can take recommendations from friends who already live in your part of Spain. I have included the details of the company we use in the further information section of this book but there are plenty of others. Your private health insurance will cover GP and hospital care and often one visit to a dental hygienist a year but will not normally cover prescriptions.

If you're relocating and are of retirement age, you need to leave the UK armed with an E121 form, also obtainable from the Department for Work and Pensions. This can be presented to the Spanish healthcare authorities and you will be entitled to free or low-cost healthcare in the same way as that of a Spanish pensioner. Whatever route you decide to follow, healthcare provision is absolutely vital whatever your age.

'How do I register with a local doctor?'

If you're part of the Spanish security system, either because you're working and paying contributions or you're retired, you can simply go to your nearest surgery and sign on. Some surgeries have more sophisticated facilities and are also *ambulatorios* (walk-in emergency facilities) but some are far more basic and will just have the services of several doctors and a practice nurse. In many of the coastal areas, where there is a large expat population, the GP might have the services of a translator should you need this. In more rural areas (and in some coastal areas) the local doctor is unlikely to speak English and in reality, why should he? In addition, in more rural areas, there is unlikely to be a translator on hand in the GP surgery. If you're in the private sector take recommendations from friends or neighbours as to the best private GP in the area.

The queues in the public sector are no better than they are in the UK. This is why many British retirees in Spain still consult a private GP who speaks English - the cost is generally €20 to €30 per consultation, payable on the spot by cash or credit card and less than the cost of a meal out for two. If they require hospital care they can access the excellent public facilities as long as they have registered with their E121. Private and state healthcare work side by side in Spain.

 ### 'How do I register my child at school?'

Education is compulsory in Spain between the ages of 6-16 years, so you need to visit the nearest local school as soon as possible following your arrival to register your children. If you feel that your Spanish might not be up to this task, visit the school with someone who does speak Spanish because the chances are the staff in the school will not speak English.

 ### 'What should I do about my car?'

The simplest advice I could give to anyone is to sell any British registered car before you move permanently to Spain. It will

185

be much simpler in the future and it would be better and safer to drive a left-hand drive vehicle. Therefore, buy a Spanish registered vehicle after you move.

If your property is to be used primarily as a holiday home at least in the short term, legally you can drive your EU registered vehicle to Spain and use it for up to six months of the year without re-registering it with Spanish plates. For the other six months it should be garaged and officially off the main road, although many cars are not. You will initially be covered by your insurance from your country of origin on a Green Card. You don't need a Green Card if you're only travelling within the European Economic Area (EEA) because if you're insured in one of those countries you are automatically covered for basic third-party liability. However, it's a good idea to carry a Green Card as it's recognisable in all countries as proof of third-party liability cover.

If the car is in Spain for more than six months per year, you should ideally register and insure it in Spain. Problems begin to arise when you leave the car in Spain all year round and never drive it back to the UK. If the car is older, it will need an MOT certificate so that you can renew your UK insurance and vehicle registration, but this certificate can only be obtained in Britain so you would have to drive it back for an MOT. The Spanish equivalent, the *Inspección Técnica de Vehículos/ITV* is not generally recognised by UK insurance companies.

Some international insurance companies will recognise the *ITV* and organise insurance while at the same time taking into account your no claims discount from your UK company. Some of these companies advertise in the English-language newspapers and magazines in Spain but do shop around for the best quote. If you move to the Costa del Sol you will also find a range of insurance companies in Gibraltar.

There are many UK expats who live in Spain all year round and continue to drive their UK registered cars, possibly illegally. Many of these cars may not have a valid *ITV* certificate or valid insurance. You can also find places which buy and sell cars on UK plates because there is a market for such vehicles. In the past, the Spanish traffic police have been fairly lenient towards the drivers of these cars but during the last few years they have tightened up considerably, particularly in the major coastal resorts. They are regularly stopping drivers with foreign plates to check that their paperwork is in order. It has become increasingly difficult to get away with simply saying that you move back and forth to your home country on a regular basis when that is not actually true.

The police can ask for proof and this can be difficult because your passport is not stamped on exit and entry into EU countries. The only proof you could provide is an airline ticket or ferry receipts. The police can also ask for proof that the car is insured in its country of origin and that the MOT is valid. If the MOT is old they will be very suspicious. Spanish law states that any car driven on Spanish roads that is more than four years old, must have a UK MOT or the Spanish equivalent, the *ITV* in order to be legal. If you can't prove that you have only been in Spain for six months, you have no insurance and no MOT, the fines can be very high. You will then have to re-register the car in Spain or take it out of the country.

Spanish law also demands that the car registration documents, the *ITV* certificate, the insurance certificate and the receipt to show you have paid the car tax should be carried in the car at all times. If you don't like the idea of keeping these documents in the car you can visit the notary and, for a fee, he will provide you with a certified copy of the documents which you can then leave in your car.

'What car taxes will I have to pay?'

The situation in Spain is somewhat different from that in the UK. Car taxes on Spanish registered cars are imposed by the local authority and not by central government. This tax, called the *Impuesto sobre Vehículos de Tracción Mecánica/IVTM*, was originally a flat rate tax across the country but now each local authority is allowed to charge whatever they like so it is impossible to say how much it will be. It depends on where you live.

The tax is based on the power of the car and on average it will be between €50 for a very small car up to €200 a year for a large vehicle. This is one more tax which you should arrange to pay by direct debit since failure to pay on the due date incurs a fine of 5–20 per cent depending on the delay in paying. However, if you pay it early or within a certain period, you will be entitled to a reduction. Your Town Hall can help you with more information.

It's very important to remember that if you sell your car, you must cancel the direct debit immediately. We have received tax demands on a car sold two years earlier because, despite the fact that we did everything correctly, the staff at the Town Hall didn't change the data on the computer. We were told to simply ignore the request for payment of the tax and eventually they would work it out.

There is, however, one anomaly in terms of car tax; should you decide to continue to run a UK registered vehicle this will not qualify for Spanish car tax even though you have insurance (compulsory by law) and a Spanish ITV this vehicle cannot be recognised by the DVLA in Swansea so you cannot pay British road tax. and you cannot pay car tax in Spain so you are essentially illegal.

'Do I need a Spanish driving licence?'

If you're a genuine tourist visiting Spain you can legally drive on the licence issued in your country of origin for up to six months.

Beyond this the situation becomes more complicated in law. If you are an EU citizen but are officially non-resident in Spain, it's a good idea to have an International Driving Permit (IDP), although it's no longer compulsory within the EU. You should also have an official translation of your driving licence and a *Certificado de Equivalencia*, a Certificate of Equivalence issued by the Spanish equivalent of the RAC. If you do not have these documents you could be fined up to €300.

If you're an EU citizen and officially resident in Spain, you can continue to use your original licence, but you should visit the nearest *Jefatura Provincial de Tráfico* (provincial traffic headquarters) where your licence will be registered in the Spanish list of drivers.

Alternatively you can exchange your current licence for a Spanish licence at the same office.

'What do I need to do to make sure I'm paying my local taxes?'

This is something which your estate agent should be able to help you with, the best solution is to visit the local Town

Hall and register yourself to pay the *IBI* by direct debit from your Spanish bank account. You can then forget about this tax because it will be collected automatically each year.

 ## 'How do I apply for planning permission?'

Planning permission and building licences should be applied for at your local Town Hall but you should have a good command of Spanish or take a translator who can help you. The application documents will need to be completed in Spanish and must be accompanied by detailed plans drawn up by an architect. There are two kinds of building licence, depending on the type of work you intend to carry out: *Licencia de obras majores* (licence for major work) and *Licencia de obras menores* (licence for small works). Your architect can help you determine which kind of licence you should apply for. If you're proposing to make alterations to a property in an urbanisation you should also obtain planning permission from the committee and the President of the urbanisation.

'Can I start work on the property before I receive my permission?'

You can start but I would not recommend it. You might be refused planning permission and have to undo all the work which you have already done. In the past this was not so much of a problem and you could simply continue to live in your 'illegal' property, but during the last few years, things have begun to change quite dramatically. The government is far less tolerant about property which does not have the correct planning permission and there are more and more reports of owners who are suddenly faced with bulldozers moving in to demolish their home.

'Should I hire an architect and how much will this cost?'

If you're planning a major renovation you must have an architect. The Town Hall will not accept plans unless they have been prepared by an architect. If you're planning a new-build you will certainly need an architect. Fees will depend on the individual project and should be negotiated case by case. Your estate agent, your lawyer or your *gestor* should be able to recommend a suitable person. I would personally recommend an English-speaking Spanish architect who is familiar with the regulations concerning Spanish property. There are British architects working in Spain and they can be found advertising in the English-language newspapers but you may find that the Town Hall will only accept plans drawn up by a Spanish architect. In the end, it may cost you more to hire a British architect because they will have to work alongside local advisers.

'Should I appoint a project manager?'

Whatever property you buy, coastal or inland, unless you speak fluent Spanish and can be on site every day keeping an eye on proceedings, I would suggest that you try to find a bilingual project manager. You can find one either by word-of-mouth recommendation or your architect may be able to advise you. A good project manager will have good contacts with local tradesmen who fully understand the way Spanish properties are built. You will find that the hourly rates of Spanish contractors are far more economical than those from your home country. Their work will usually be of a high standard and the project manager will be able to take your brief and convert it into a brief for the local tradesmen and craftsmen. A good project manager is really worth his fee and you will probably end up paying less than if you try and organise operations yourself.

'How do I go about finding suitable tradesmen to carry out the work required?'

If you decide to take charge of everything yourself there are two routes you can follow, the first is to use the services of local Spanish tradesmen either from word-of-mouth recommendations or via the local yellow pages, I have provided the Spanish term for many of these tradesmen in the glossary for this chapter. I am making the assumption that many of the readers of this book do not speak fluent Spanish therefore all you need to know is one question *'¿Habla Inglés?'* (Do you speak English?). If the answer is 'No', move to the next telephone number. You should remember that if you don't speak reasonably fluent Spanish, it will be virtually impossible to be your own project manager. Most Spanish tradesmen don't speak fluent English - and why should they? If they do speak some English this can lead to misunderstandings and things not being done the way you want them. Another good reason to employ a bilingual project manager. Then you get the best of both worlds.

Many British expats in Spain take the second route and find British tradesmen who are sometimes working the black economy in Spain. They will do the work for you but often they only want to paid in cash and obviously will not issue invoices, such tradesmen are not difficult to find. Unfortunately, many are not actually qualified tradesmen, instead they are good DIY experts who are now living in Spain and trying to earn a living.

The brief is easy because the person commissioning the work speaks the same language, but often the hourly rate charged by the tradesman is equivalent to the rate which you might pay in the UK and not the rate which a Spanish tradesman would charge.

We know one friend who arrived in Spain from London and paid £1,000 just to have her living room painted! A Spanish decorator would probably have done the same job for a quarter of the price!

'What can I do if the work is not carried out to my specifications?'

Another reason to employ a competent project manager is that you will hopefully avoid getting conned either by Spanish or British 'tradesmen'. The same friend who paid the extortionate price for decorating, also employed someone to tile her kitchen. He needed an electric tile cutter to do the job so she paid for it, but when the work was completed he kept the tile cutter. Another friend wanted some major work done and actually paid the 'builder' (the son of a friend of a friend) €10,000 up front to do the work. Not only did he fail to complete the job but he also refused to reimburse the advance payment. She has no recompense in law because she did not even have a receipt for the first payment. It was all done on trust!

The other downside to using British or Spanish tradesmen who work on the black is the fact that because you will undoubtedly be asked to pay cash, you will not have an *IVA* (VAT) receipt to prove that the work was actually done. As a result, when you come to sell your property, you can't prove to the taxman that you have improved the property and hence have it deducted from your Capital Gains Tax liability. This could make a big difference with major renovations, which increase the value of the property significantly.

This is particularly important if you buy an old property in the countryside in need of total renovation. In this case, you really should use officially registered workers and receive *IVA* (VAT) receipts. I say this because extensive renovation will produce a property potentially worth a lot more than you originally paid for it so you need to be able to prove what renovations were carried out. Then you can offset the costs against your future tax bill. If you buy for €100,000, spend €100,000 on renovation and then sell for €300,000, you need to be able to prove to the taxman and the notary that your profit is only €100,000. Remember that increasing numbers of both lawyers and notaries are refusing to get involved in under-declaration of value which in the past was a way of avoiding Capital Gains Tax.

 ### 'How can I make sure the property is looked after in my absence?'

If you're not living in the property all year round, it's a good idea to find a friend locally who is prepared to hold a key on your behalf. On occasions we have held keys for up to seven apartments in our urbanisation which meant, for example, that following a storm we could check the security of the properties and avoid long-term damage. Some of these properties are let so we provide the key and are a point of contact for the tenants if they have difficulties. If you don't have someone who can do this, you need to find a local property management company and they will charge you for the service. They advertise in the local English-language newspapers.

'What should I do about the pool and the garden?'

Once more consult your neighbours first. Pools don't look after themselves and need regular maintenance and the garden also needs to be looked after. If the neighbours are unable to help, there are plenty of pool maintenance companies and gardeners who advertise in the local papers but their services will cost you money which has to be deducted from potential income.

'What should I know about letting my property?'

There are many people from northern Europe who have bought properties in Spain which they have let short-term for holiday rentals, or long-term to locals and many have done very well in the buy-to-let market. This is particularly true if the property was bought some years ago when prices were much lower. In fact rental income often paid the mortgage and the owner then benefited from what were essentially free holidays. This is less likely nowadays because property in the coastal areas is far more expensive and the rental market is shrinking as holidaymakers are increasingly choosing cheaper destinations.

Various laws exist in Spain with respect to rented property, but if you are in the process of buying property now for future rental you only need to be aware of the current laws introduced in 1995. If you buy a property with a sitting tenant you could find that this person is still covered by the old laws and they could pass the lease onto their children or even to their grandchildren. Once more get your lawyer to check everything very carefully and avoid sitting tenants like the plague! At the very best, recovering your property could take the tenant's lifetime plus two years.

The new laws introduced in 1995 provide for annual contracts for up to five years and the tenant has the right to renew the contract each year until the limit is reached. If the landlord initially grants the tenant a lease of three years, the tenant can then insist that this contract is extended for a further five years on a year by year basis. One further factor which can give the tenant more protection is if you allow the tenant to take over the utility bills or community charges. This proves that the tenant is occupying the property legally. What often happens with long-term lets is that the owner offers a contract for 11 months and then renews it if all is well. This means that a tenant effectively has none of the rights they should have as a long-term tenant and could be evicted at any time. In practice, if you're looking for a long-term let, particularly in coastal areas, you will be hard-pressed to find an owner willing to give you a contract longer than 11 months.

Letting holiday properties is not quite such a problem because the tenant does not have any rights to automatic extension of the lease. However, should you agree a short-term lease of several months and the tenant decides to stay in the property, eviction can take up to six months and during that period they may not be paying the rent. The eventual court order might call for eviction and outstanding rental payments to be made, but by this time the tenant who has caused you the problems could have disappeared.

If you only want to let you holiday property for a few weeks each year the safest way to do this is through word-of-mouth and friends. If you want to put your property into the hands of an agent, I would suggest that you use an agent based in your home country and find someone locally in Spain who will act as key holder and cleaner (for a fee). In this way the payments for the rental are made, for example, in the UK into your local bank account. You are reimbursed on a regular basis and you know who is in control of your investment. Remember that if you let your Spanish property the income should legally be declared in Spain for income tax purposes. This applies even if you are paid in sterling in the UK because the income is considered to be from Spain. If you are a non-resident, this tax is 24 per cent of every euro earned with no deductions allowed. If you are resident and letting a second property there are many deductions which can be made and you could end up paying little or no tax. It is true that many people do let their properties and say nothing to the tax authorities but the fact remains that they are breaking the law.

The alternative is to put your property into the hands of a local letting agency. The majority are very good and very trustworthy but they could charge you up to 20 per cent of the rental income as commission. Find one through good local recommendations and you will probably have no problems. The best agencies will handle cleaning, provision of bedlinen and customer service to your clients. The most important thing is that the agency has local trust and a good reputation.

Remember if you don't live in Spain you have no way of knowing whether your property is occupied (unless you have good neighbours). We know of instances where owners have turned up to stay in their own property only to find that there were tenants occupying it. The agency had not informed them that it was let for that period. If they had not turned up unexpectedly, they might never have known that the property had been rented. They might also have never received the rental income for that period.

If you let your Spanish property on an official contract on a long-term basis you will also find that the tenant has the right of first refusal if you decide to sell the property. You will be required by law to submit in writing a document which states the price and the conditions of sale. If the tenant does not accept, you are then free to sell the property to a third party. If you do not inform the tenant in advance the tenant could even have the sale annulled. This could happen even if you have not set up a formal contract but the tenant can prove from bank receipts or utilities bills that they have been paying rent for a considerable period. In Spain the tenant still has considerable protection under the law and apart from carefully controlled holiday lets you should take good legal advice before you enter into any long-term rental contracts.

'What happens if I decide to sell my property?'

If you decide that you have made the wrong decision or that you simply want to move on to another property, there is no problem in selling. You can select a local agent but this agent should ideally specialise in local property. You can also sell privately and then put your lawyer in contact with the buyer's lawyer or you could sell through a UK based agent, an Internet-based estate agent or property portal.

'What are the financial implications of selling the property?'

If you decide to sell up and move to another area or find an alternative property, it's important to establish what costs will be involved. Let's take an example of a property you bought for €200,000. The purchase costs for this would be around €20,000 (10 per cent). So if you decide a year later that you want to sell what would this cost you if you manage to sell your property at €220,000?

- Estate agent's fee would be €11,000.
- Capital Gains Tax - Rates are now 18 per cent of profits for both residents and non-residents and you don't pay any if you buy another property of similar value. Assume 18 per cent of €20,000 = €3,600.

As you can see, these costs alone reduce your profit considerably. This is all before you've included the costs of removal, improvements and any redecoration which you felt was needed. Our removal from the UK to Spain, for example cost €4,500. Redecoration or improvements to the property could easily add another €5,000 or more.

So if you sell after a year you would really need a capital appreciation of around 30 per cent just to break even on the buying and selling costs which, after a short period, is just not realistic. If you have to sell at the original buying price, or even less, you would be seriously out of pocket especially after paying 10–12 per cent buying costs on your next property. This is why it's really important you're absolutely sure you're making the right decision before you purchase the property.

'What should I do to ensure that my interests are taken into account?'

Very simply, you should register to vote in Spanish local elections. You may not be able to vote in the national elections but you can vote in the local elections and the European elections. I have been struck by the number of expats who complain incessantly about uncontrolled development, lack of facilities such as post offices, schools and all the other things required for modern life but all they do is to complain to fellow expats over coffee or something stronger at their local bar. Empty complaints achieve nothing but voting can change things.

Many do not realise that if you are an EU citizen who spends more than six months of the year in your chosen property within the EU, you have the democratic right to a vote in municipal elections. You also have the right to be elected to office although to do this successfully you would of course have to speak fluent Spanish to take part in the council meetings. There are already expats who are elected representatives in local governments on the Costa Blanca and on the Costa del Sol. Many of the smaller political parties are already canvassing the votes of the expat community but some are fighting a losing battle because many expats are not registered to vote.

The first step is to visit your local Town Hall with your passport and proof that you live in the local area. Utility bills, tax bills, your rental contract or your *escritura* will be accepted and then you can arrange to have yourself entered into the local *padrón*, the voter's list. It's important to be on this list anyway because local infrastructure, facilities and amenities are allocated according to the number of registered inhabitants. Once you have registered, you will be given a certificate to prove that you are on the list. The local Town Hall is generally very happy to register as many inhabitants as possible because this could give them a bigger slice of the cake from central government funds which are based on the total number of registered voters. It's in their interests to have as many voters registered as possible but they also need these voters to vote for them if they are going to stay in power.

Theoretically registering to vote in local elections also gives you the right to vote for the Member of the European Parliament (MEP) representing your part of Spain. This is true if you only choose to register to vote in Spain. However, you can also register to vote in your previous constituency in the UK for up to 15 years after you leave. You will then have a vote (by post or by proxy) in any UK election and you can then choose whether your European vote should be cast in Spain or in the UK. The local Spanish Town Hall should contact you prior to a European election to ask where you would like your vote to be recorded. You can't vote in both countries and if your vote is recorded in Spain you don't have to vote for a Spanish MEP.

I also feel very strongly about the need for British expats to register to vote in their old UK constituency because it will also give them a vote in any European referenda (or General Election) which might be called in the future. You can do this for up to 15 years from the date of departure from the UK. Expats might vote differently compared with those people still living in the UK. For example, many expats would probably vote for the euro to be adopted in Britain. Those of us who have chosen to live in Europe might also vote differently on the European Constitution.

Summary

- What immediate steps should I take?
- What should I do about transfer of utility services?
- What should I do about medical care?
- What should I do about my car?
- I plan to renovate my property - what steps should I take?
- I want to build a new property - is this difficult?
- What should I know about letting my property?
- Do I have democratic rights in Spain?

Glossary

ambulatoria	walk-in minor emergency facility in some surgeries
Empadronimiento/Padron	the voter's list
'¿Habla Inglés?'	Do you speak English?
Impuesto sobre Vehículos de Tracción Mecánica/IVTM	Spanish road tax
Inspección Técnica de Vehículos/ITV	Spanish equivalent of the MOT
Jefatura Provincial de Tráfico	provincial traffic headquarters
Licencia de obras majores	licence for major work
Licencia de obras menores	licence for small works
Telefónica	the Spanish equivalent of British Telecom

Tradesmen and services

arquitecto	architect
arquitecto de jardines	landscape gardener
carpintero	carpenter
constructor	builder

electricista	electrician
jardinero	gardener
pintor	painter
fontanero	plumber

And finally...

A move to Spain could be the best move you could ever make in your life. You would be escaping many of the features of modern-day Britain which can make life increasingly depressing; overcrowding, political correctness, increasing taxes, increasing crime (despite what the Government says), and a relatively high cost of living.

In Spain, if you choose to live in the coastal areas like many expats do, you will find yourself surrounded by many others who have made the decision to move for exactly the same reasons as your own, and you will rapidly make many new friends. There will probably be no need to learn the language, although I think that we should because it gives us many more opportunities to really enjoy Spanish life and is only polite to our hosts as we begin a new life in their country.

If you choose to move to inland Spain you really need to consider the fact that you will be living in what may be a very rural area. It's rather like moving from a British suburban environment to the highlands of Scotland, the Yorkshire moors, or to the centre of Wales. For many this is absolute paradise but others could feel very isolated even if you were to move just 100 kilometres inland from the coast.

Buying property in Spain is not as simple as the TV relocation programmes would have you believe, it can be frustrating. The bureaucracy is different and on occasions can seem to take forever, but the problems can be resolved if you have the right people advising you, like a good lawyer, and you have done your homework. You have taken a step in the right direction by reading this book, but many potential expatriates do no homework at all.

We left the UK in 2001 and now we could not imagine going back. Nowhere in the world can be called a perfect location but Spain certainly ticks most of the boxes.

Addendum 1:

The *escritura* (Spanish title deeds) explained

The *Escritura Pública* is the new document that you sign at the Notary's office and which goes to the Property Registry.

The first few paragraphs deal with the vendor (*parte vendedor* or *vendedora*) and their legal details, passport number and address. Then there is a description of the buyer (*parte comprador* or *compradora*) with passport numbers and other identification. Note that all male sellers will be designated *Don* and females are *Doña*.

The next section describes the property either as an *apartamento* (apartment) or *vivienda unifamiliar* (house) with all the legal details but most importantly the description. This section of the document describes the floor area in *metros cuadrados* (square metres) split into *superficie útil* (habitable surface area) and *superficie construida* (the total built e area including terraces and the *elementos communes* (common areas) linked to the property should it be an apartment in an urbanisation.

The document then describes the rooms which you will be buying; here are the translations:

hall	hall
cocina	kitchen
salon-comedor	literally lounge-dining room, often just a living room
dormitorios	bedrooms
terraza	terrace or balcony
cuarto de baño	bathroom

If the property is in an urbanisation, the next section describes the *linderos* (neighbouring properties) and the share of *cuota* (community charges) applied to the property.

The *escritura* will then go on to describe where the property is registered, who has the title deed to the land, the legal charges on the property and the *Referencia catastral* (the entry in the Spanish Property Register).

The next section of the document provides the number for the *Referencia catastral* and under the heading *Información Registral* confirms that the vendor is entitled to sell. To fully understand this you need your lawyer to explain it unless you speak fluent Spanish.

We then come to the part of the document with the title *estipulaciones* (conditions). The vendor and the buyer are named along with the official price, confirmation that all bills have been paid, that there are no present occupants and, if the vendor is a non-resident, that 3 per cent of the purchase price will be retained by the notary against unpaid taxes.

Finally the document contains the signatures of all sellers and the buyers, countersigned by the notary. A copy of the *nota simple* may also be attached to the *escritura*.

Addendum 2:

Further information

I have provided further information on companies or services which I know from first-hand experience, but that doesn't mean there aren't lots of other great resources available. Even so, take extreme care and check the reliability of information you find on the Internet. Although there is no shortage of information, much of it is written by those with a vested interest in selling you property, such as a developer or estate agent. If you check all the facts and research well in advance of your property search and purchase, the experience will be a lot easier and far more rewarding.

Books

There are many books and magazines on the market which are an attempt to cash in on the popularity of buying property abroad, along with a plethora of TV programmes. In many instances the authors have never lived in the countries concerned, and their information has been gleaned from research, rather than first-hand experience. Such information is not necessarily wrong – but it can occasionally be inaccurate. Here is a selection of books which I have found useful:

Hampshire, David *Buying a Home in Spain* (2006, Survival Books). This is the latest edition, the earlier edition was my bible when I moved to Spain.

King, Harry *Buying a Property in Spain* (2002, How to Books)

King, Harry *Going to Live in Spain* (2003, How to Books)

Provan, Tom *Going to Live on the Costa del Sol* (2004, How to Books)

Provan, Tom *We've Gone to Spain* (2006, How to Books)

Searle, David *You and the Law in Spain* (2006, Santana Books)
   This is the latest edition and a wonderful source of information on Spanish law.

Further addresses, useful information and websites

Please note that before providing any information below on private companies I asked for their permission to do so.

Removals

If you are moving to Spain and you want to use a Spanish based removal company I can thoroughly recommend the following firm having used them:
Union Jack Removals, (www.union-jack-removals.co.uk, UK free phone number 0800 0361011).

Health insurance in Spain

When you first move to Spain your healthcare should be covered by the E106 form available from the Department for Work and Pensions in the UK. When this expires, unless you are legally working in Spain and contributing to social security you will need to organise private healthcare. We had superb service from Medifiati and I can recommend them to anyone, but there are others.

Medifiati (part of FIATC Seguros), www.fiatc.es, (website only in Spanish)

Anyone contemplating a move to Spain should check out the healthcare information on the Department for Work and Pensions website: **www.dwp.gov.uk**, or you can get advice by telephoning 0191 218 7777.

Useful websites

www.defra.gov.uk/animal/quarantine - information about the export of pet animals.

www.dss.gov.uk - information about UK state pensions and pension forecasts.

www.fsa.gov.uk - official website of the Financial Services Authority for advice on financial planning.

www.inlandrevenue.gov.uk - the site for information on organising your tax affairs when you leave the UK.

www.naric.org.uk - the website for NARIC which provides information and advice on the compatibility of UK professional qualifications and their recognition abroad.

www.ukinspain.com British Embassy in Spain.

Index

Edited by Simon Noxon

DICTIONARY
OF
SPANISH BUILDING TERMS

With an Introduction to Construction and Renovation in Spain

SPANISH–ENGLISH
ENGLISH–SPANISH

summersdale

DICTIONARY OF SPANISH BUILDING TERMS

Edited by Simon Noxon

£12.99   Paperback   ISBN: 978 1 84024 661 2

This dictionary contains essential language for homeowners or tradesmen maintaining or renovating property in Spain.

- Accessible and comprehensive, the most up-to-date and easy-to-use dictionary of Spanish building terms

- Includes hundreds of technical words you won't find in an ordinary dictionary

- Covers tools and equipment for every aspect of construction, carpentry, decorating, ironmongery, metalwork, plumbing and heating

- Also includes terminology for financial and property matters

Whether you own property or work in Spain, this book will help you to communicate and avoid costly misunderstandings. Comprehensive and easy to use, this is one book you won't want to be without.

Spain
by the horns

A journey to the heart of a culture

TIM ELLIOTT

SPAIN BY THE HORNS
A Journey to the Heart of a Culture

Tim Elliott

£7.99   Paperback   ISBN: 978 1 84024 574 5

It all began when Tim read a newspaper story about a bullfighter who was spotted practising on the beach at dawn. Intrigued, Tim tracked him down, looking for an interview, but instead he was told about another bullfighter in Spain, Jesulín, a man described as 'perhaps one of the most controversial and ridiculously over the top characters you're likely to meet'.

Disillusioned with his current life and job, Tim went to Spain to find him. Criss-crossing a country synonymous with flamboyance, passion, spontaneity and adventure, Tim found himself in a world of ancient ritual and eccentric characters, on a quixotic quest through a land where no one was ever on time but where every vibrant second oozed with the promise of heat and excitement. The famous bullfighter, who filled arenas with adoring women, surely held the key to the heart of this fiery nation.

Funny, fast-paced and revealing, *Spain by the Horns* takes you below the surface of a nation on a journey to the heart of a culture.

Tim Elliott is an award-winning journalist and author of *The Bolivian Times*.

'Traversing Spain on a diet of tapas and sherry, Elliott finds a world of ancient ritual, eccentric characters and all-consuming passions. The result is a delight'
WEEKEND GOLD COAST BULLETIN

'Like Hemingway and many others before him, Elliott knows that to understand bullfighting is to understand Spain itself... Elliott is both an amiable guide and a first class writer, and, as always, the joy lies in the journey'
THE BULLETIN

A Lizard in my Luggage

MAYFAIR TO MALLORCA IN ONE EASY MOVE

ANNA NICHOLAS

A LIZARD IN MY LUGGAGE
Mayfair to Mallorca in One Easy Move

Anna Nicholas

£7.99   Paperback   ISBN: 978 1 84024 565 3

Anna, a PR consultant to Mayfair's ritziest and most glamorous, had always thought Mallorca was for the disco and beer-swilling fraternity. That was until her sister hired an au pair from a rural part of the island who said it was the most beautiful place on earth. On a visit, Anna impulsively decided to buy a ruined farmhouse.

Despite her fear of flying, she kept a foot in both camps and commuted to central London to manage her PR company. But she found herself drawn away from the bustle and stress of life in the fast lane towards a more tranquil existence.

Told with piquant humour, *A Lizard in my Luggage* explores Mallorca's fiestas and traditions, as well as the ups and downs of living in a rural retreat. It is about learning to appreciate the simple things and take risks in pursuit of real happiness. Most importantly, it shows that life can be lived between two places.

'A beautifully written and highly entertaining account of the upside of downshifting'

THE DAILY MIRROR

'If you thought that glitz and glamour don't mix with rural country living you must read this book'

Bella Online

'An enjoyable read for anyone wanting to live their dream'

Lynne Franks, broadcaster and author

'A hugely entertaining and witty account of how to juggle life and work between two countries, keep fit and stay sane!'

Col. John Blashford-Snell, OBE, author and explorer

www.summersdale.com